The Counter Reformation

Religion and society in early modern Europe

Martin D. W. Jones
Head of History
Brighton College

CAMBRIDGE
UNIVERSITY PRESS

For Jenny

Published by the Press Syndicate of the University of Cambridge
The Pitt Building, Trumpington Street, Cambridge CB2 1RP
40 West 20th Street, New York, NY 10011-4211, USA
10 Stamford Road, Oakleigh, Melbourne 3166, Australia

© Cambridge University Press 1995

First published 1995

Printed in Great Britain at the University Press, Cambridge

A catalogue record for this book is available from the British Library

Library of Congress cataloging in publication data
Jones, Martin D. W.
The Counter-Reformation: religion and society in early modern Europe / Martin D.W. Jones.
      p.   cm. – (Cambridge topics in history)
Includes index.
1. Counter Reformation. 2. Europe Church history. I Title. II. Series.
BR430.J65   1995
274'. 06 – dc20   94-28877   CIP

ISBN 0 521 43993 0   paperback

Cover illustration: The Madonna of the Rosary by Caravaggio,
Kunsthistorisches Museum, Vienna

Acknowledgements
The author and publisher are grateful for permission to reproduce extracts and illustrations.
Extracts are acknowledged at the end of each source.
9, by permission of the British Library, London; 12, 13, The National Gallery, London;
14, Giraudon/Bridgeman Art Library; 22, Witt Library, Courtauld Institute of Art;
113, INDEX/Bridgeman Art Library; 114, The Metropolitan Museum of Art, Gift of Mr & Mrs
Charles Wrightsman, 1978 (1978.517); 161, all rights reserved © Museo del Prado, Madrid
Every effort has been made to reach copyright holders. The publisher would like to hear from
anyone whose rights they have unwittingly infringed.

Picture research by Callie Kendall

The development of this book owes much to the meticulous care of my editor and the stimulating
criticism of my series editor Richard Brown. John Morrill and Bob Scribner both read the type-
script, made valued suggestions and saved me from various errors. Glyn Redworth kindly gave me
8.7(b). Trevor Davies offered invaluable aid with translations. Two very special debts must be
recorded. As I owe my fascination with this subject to the lectures of Jack Scarisbrick so it is only
because of Jenny that this book exists.

LD

Contents

Introduction

For centuries, the medieval church was painted as rotten to the core and its survival in the face of Protestant onslaught put down to the iron-grip ruthlessness of inquisitors, strident Jesuits, warrior popes and kings like Philip II. The story of the Counter Reformation seemed dry as dust, devoid of glamour, of heroes, of virtue. Forty years of research have turned that impression upside down and completely altered our understanding of key elements of early modern Europe. Much still remains to be sorted out, but this book presents some of the revolutionary fruit of that work and the new synthesis which is emerging.

Scholars have transformed the very meaning of the term 'Counter Reformation'. It was coined originally by late 18th-century German Protestants to label those aggressive, often successful Catholic campaigns waged from about 1550 to about 1650 to check the growth of Protestantism and to recover lands and people lost to the heretics. The concept defined the Roman church as reacting to its enemies, classified Catholic initiatives as negative and made Protestantism responsible for halting and then reversing the decline of the medieval church. Luther had saved the papacy. Needless to say, such an interpretation was unattractive to Catholic scholars who, seeking to emphasise a positive image of independent self-renewal, suggested instead 'Catholic Reformation', occasionally 'Catholic Renaissance'. The problem was that Reformation-era history was itself corrupt, its practitioners agents working for one side or the other. Only in the last forty years has historical scholarship broken free. As the long shadows of partisan bias have receded, a different landscape is being revealed and the old term 'Counter Reformation' has been found so inappropriate that few now use it without major qualification.

The first two chapters of this book sample late medieval religious belief and institutions. Alongside the ignorance and corruption so well known, there was also a growing personal piety and structural reform. Our late medieval ancestors were engaged in a religious quest. Their impulses created and focused powerful spiritual movements. We must recognise their religious vitality, for continuity from the 15th century was so strong that, without an understanding of the late medieval situation, we will have no base for reference and comparison. And for that, the first thing we have to do is discard traditional notions of a church in terminal decline. Chapter 3 then turns to examine the failure of initial institutional moves against Luther and to assess why most early efforts to halt the spreading Reformation were equally unsuccessful. This is a story little told and still under-researched, yet there was nothing inevitable about it. Because scholars judge the Counter Reformation to have begun with the Roman Inquisition in 1542, Trevor-Roper's phrase 'anti-Reformation' is used to describe these earlier offensives.

The Council of Trent is the focus of Chapter 4. Trent has always been regarded as fundamental to the story of Catholic recovery. By defining doctrine and condemning heresy, it sorted out precisely what was 'truth'. Second, it passed a series of new laws to remove abuses and revitalise the clergy. For both, the Council is justly famous. But how easily and how universally would those changes be accomplished? Unenforced laws are worthless, yet it is only recently that historians have tried to measure the effectiveness of these legendary reform decrees – the subject of Chapters 5 to 7. Chapter 5 looks at institutions and starts by considering the development of a supreme papal monarchy. Hierarchical authority, especially in wartime, can stifle innovation and a tension between creativity and conformity will be observed throughout the sources in this book. The latter part of Chapter 5 examines that conflict set within the notable recovery of monastic vitality. At the same time, it demonstrates something of the frontier research now undertaken – in this case, feminist religious history.

Chapters 6 and 7 assess the progress of front-line reform among clergy and people in the parishes. Developments in religion receive little attention here, although the first part of Chapter 7 tackles the rich panorama of beliefs and practice which scholars uncomfortably term 'popular religion'. The religious controversies of the 16th century trained a strong spotlight on the beliefs and practices of the people. What people believed mattered now in a way quite unknown to the Middle Ages. Reformers of both sides, trying to impose articles of belief requiring intellectual and personal assent, came into contact with 'a massive presence they could neither recognise nor accept as Christianity' (Ginzburg, 1979): alongside and beyond official religion lay a broad swathe of popular folklore, conjurations and invocations. Historians disagree about the meaning of the term 'popular religion' and, to a large degree, their disagreements flow from the debate about whether medieval Christianity was shot through with 'semi-paganism'.

These two chapters are constructed to reflect the balance of research which, led by Jean Delumeau and John Bossy, focuses no longer on institutions but on the interaction of religion and society at the local level. Reformers called for the creation of a godly society. Charity and morality were of as much interest as church attendance. The programme was enormously ambitious, beyond the capacity of church authority alone. However much was actually achieved (and currently that remains very uncertain), the active participation of the secular state, equally concerned with discipline and order, was a prerequisite. By definition, such calls to virtue could not be accomplished overnight so these chapters also demonstrate why the long-held belief that Catholic renewal was all over by 1610 (or, at the very latest, 1648) must be abandoned. The timescale has to be pushed forward, even for Italy, to cover the entire 17th century; for France and the Empire, the impact of renewal peaked in the early 18th century. Indeed, so slow was reform that Philip Hoffman (1984) believes 'Catholic Reformations' (in the plural) to be a more accurate title.

Running underneath these chapters are two critical theological currents. Trent firmly rejected the Protestant notion that people were incapable of co-operating with God in their own salvation. It also gave strong encouragement to 'Thomism', the teachings of St Thomas Aquinas (d. 1274). The clergy's active involvement in the debate about begging, examined in Chapter 6, arose naturally from Trent's insistence on individual responsibility. The doubts about witchcraft discussed in Chapter 7 were influenced by Thomist insistence that everything operated according to divinely established laws. The defence of Indian rights in America, another topic in Chapter 7, sprang equally from a Thomist perspective. When reformist Catholic clergy championed such causes, they fought for more than social justice. They fought for theological orthodoxy against the same heresies propagated by Protestants.

Only in the final chapter is the traditional Counter Reformation examined – a reflection of the transformation wrought by recent research. The Catholic revival militant took many guises. Three varieties are sampled here: the vicious internal struggle in Spain to keep itself heresy-free; the gentle but nonetheless spectacular recovery of Catholic primacy in the religious borderlands of the Empire, achieved through the preaching and teaching of Jesuits; and the ambiguous behaviour of that archetypal Counter Reformation warrior, Philip II. Any idea that popes and Spanish monarchs formed a united front, the backbone of the Counter Reformation, is challenged by the appalling relationship between Rome and Madrid. Further, the second part of Chapter 8 considers the momentous clash of sovereignties between the papacy and the Venetian Republic that erupted in 1605. The interplay of church and state was an issue of the age, not a by-product of Protestantism.

Scholars now suggest that the Protestant Reformation and the Catholic Reformation were sisters, or perhaps cousins: 'two different outcomes of the general aspiration towards religious regeneration which pervaded late 15th and early 16th century Europe' (Evennett, 1968). There was one reformation, built on rising clerical standards and lay expectations, but several solutions to the problem of how best to revive the church and religious practice, to raise spiritual and moral standards, to make doctrine clearer. We must be careful. Doctrine, not abuses, was the real issue between Protestants and Catholics: 'Even had Rome observed her religion with the zeal of the hermits, her false doctrine must still have been overthrown' (Luther, 1535). Was theological rift inevitable? Catholics and Protestants did, after all, agree a theology of salvation at Regensburg in 1541 – examined in the final part of Chapter 3. Historical 'might-have-beens' are seductive. Yet to his death, Luther insisted on calling the Catholic church 'our mother who nourished us with word and sacrament and taught us the faith' (1543). In a complete reversal of position, modern theologians now suggest that Luther was more Catholic than his Catholic opponents. Perhaps we need to see the reform movements as a delta. Certainly we need to recognise their common source.

Even so, we have to accept that Protestants and Catholics did split apart, that this is a story of alienation and that a 400-year 'cold war' had begun. We also have to recognise that the Catholic church was deeply affected by that split. The shock of Protestant dissent and revolt proved the catalyst which made reform more earnest, more urgent. The rapid spread of Protestantism altered the pace and direction of change. Reform was under way well before 1517, but how successful it would have been we shall never know for it was overtaken in its adolescence by the great crisis of the Reformation. The defeat of those Catholics who believed in justification by faith and prayed for reunion with Protestants (Chapter 3) meant from the 1540s that 'the Catholic revival unequivocally assumed the form of the Counter Reformation' (Fenlon, 1972). For a time, the direction and shape of internal reform was determined primarily by the pressures imposed by the Reformation. At the same time, the Counter Reformation itself 'gained increased cogency as internal reform proceeded' (Evennett, 1965). By 1700, however, Counter Reformation had waned. Everywhere it was the pastoral and spiritual renewal of the Catholic world that stood proud. This book is titled *The Counter Reformation* only because the term is so instantly recognised. As you will discover, it rarely appears after this page.

The documents

We find it difficult to grasp why theology could tear peoples apart. If we pretend that theology was irrelevant and try to make the story work without it, we will never make sense of medieval and early modern Europe. Ideas are central to every culture. An understanding of history can only be based on an appreciation of the values of the people who lived in the past. I have thus included a generous slice of theology. Don't be alarmed. Concepts are explained and you will soon master the jargon – for that is *all* it is. Finally, remember that the extracts come from people deeply involved in controversy. Most were unable and unwilling to look objectively. But it is their very subjective perspective that historians need to study. Many of the documents have been translated especially for this book (they are marked † at the end of the citation), using a free style which nonetheless keeps to the spirit and meaning of the original. Spelling has also been modernised. Early modern sentences can be difficult to follow. If you have problems, read the extract aloud; that usually does the trick.

The cover

Caravaggio's *Madonna of the Rosary* (*c.* 1605–7) illustrates significant themes within the Catholic and Counter Reformations. Tradition said that the rosary was given to St Dominic by the Virgin Mary who promised to favour all who would use her aid to prayer. St Teresa of Avila called it 'a chain uniting Heaven and Earth', and here the Virgin presides as her saint distributes her gift to a varied and eager group. To the right, the famed preacher St Peter Martyr invites the viewer also to accept the double offer. But these were two Dominican saints who had battled hard against heresy in the 13th century. As St Dominic had used the rosary then to enlist divine aid so St Peter summons the viewer now to take it up in the fight against Protestantism. The Virgin and her rosary became a battle standard of the Counter Reformation.

References

H. O. Evennett, 'The Counter-Reformation' in *The Reformation Crisis*, ed. J. Hurstfield, Edward Arnold, 1965
C. Ginzburg, 'Cheese and Worms, The Cosmos of a Sixteenth-Century Miller' in *Religion and the People, 800–1700*, ed. J. Obelkevich, University of North Carolina Press, 1979
P. T. Hoffman, *Church and Community in the Diocese of Lyon, 1500–1789*, Yale University Press, 1984

For Evennett (1968) and Fenlon, see *Suggestions for further reading*.

1 Varieties of belief: late medieval religion and the people

Decadent popes presiding over a church theologically bankrupt, peddling a pseudo-religion of superstition to an ignorant and credulous population: this is the all-too-familiar image of Catholicism on the eve of the Reformation. Old perspectives die hard, but our understanding of the church and the service it provided has been revolutionised. No longer can we see either church or religion as being in terminal decline. As long ago as 1929, Lucien Febvre argued that this era 'had an immense appetite for the divine'. Late medieval urban congregations complained loudly if a priest did not celebrate a mass and both a morning and an evening service daily. From the early 14th century, our ancestors had been involved in an urgent 'pursuit of holiness' and it is with that vibrancy this book must begin, examining what historians call 'modes of spirituality'. Without it, the subsequent story will possess neither roots nor context.

The fundamental issue under investigation here is the degree to which late medieval religion served the needs of its customers. Was theirs merely a pragmatic religion, a matter of sensible insurance against the inevitability of death, fear of hell and the penalties of divine judgement? How far did it enable people to satisfy, through ritual, their deepest impulses? Did it set minds at peace? As you read the extracts, remember a number of problems. First, while rising literacy meant that some members of the late medieval urban laity could live a more active religious life than any for a thousand years, most remained illiterate and so are unable to speak to us now of their hopes and fears. Can we penetrate the silence of the sources? Second, medieval religious uniformity was only superficial. Attitudes and values varied significantly from region to region. Can we draw valid generalisations? Third, there were many levels of religious experience: emotional and intellectual, active and passive, popular and elitist. Some historians classify certain medieval beliefs and practices as 'superstitious' or 'pagan'. Yet it is false to judge lay piety by the standards and expectations of the clerical heights. Religion is a two-way process, never something simply imposed by the priests. Further, the line between 'religion' and 'magic' has 'always had a certain elasticity about it' (Thomas, 1971). Should historians presume to make so subjective a distinction? Finally, try extremely hard to forget that there was ever such a thing as the Reformation, until Chapter 3. We must not approach late medieval religion looking for clues or flaws which explain the Reformation. Such an approach presumes that something was very wrong – and thus makes the Reformation inevitable. One of the achievements of modern scholarship has been to demolish the venerable idea that people wanted the type of religion offered by the Protestants.

Death and devotion

Death and the afterlife are a preoccupation of most religions. Our medieval ancestors saw themselves as pilgrims who journeyed hopefully but uncertainly to paradise. Their pursuit of holiness was a search for salvation, but pilgrims could not know how they would fare before the inevitable judgement. Death and the need to prepare for it loomed large in their religion and its sermons, literature and art; their all-too-great familiarity with death does not seem to have blunted its impact upon them. Anxious fears for the soul's fate, of indeterminate punishment in purgatory and the eternal flames of hell troubled many a mind. Theirs was, after all, a time of troubles, of social unrest and agrarian crisis, of political strife and civil war, of the inexorable advance of the Turks: 'Crisis was the most obvious and pervasive factor in this period' (Oberman, 1974). Famine, war and disease devoured as never before. Two-thirds of children died before their tenth birthday. Most adults never reached 45. Preachers, writers and painters exploited the presence of death to goad as well as inspire. Sermons and books specifically taught people to prepare for their own death. In such circumstances, is it any wonder that they returned again and again to one haunting image: the naked dead clambering out of their graves to be judged? If we find their religion extravagant, excitable, even extreme, we would do well to remember the brooding presence of death.

1.1   Faith and fear: a plea

O come, O come, Emmanuel!
Redeem thy captive Israel,
That into exile drear is gone
Far from the face of God's dear Son.
Rejoice! Rejoice! Emmanuel
Shall come to thee, O Israel.   5

O come, thou Branch of Jesse! draw
The quarry from the lion's claw;
From the dread caverns of the grave,
From nether hell thy people save.   10

O come, O come, thou Dayspring bright!
Pour on our souls thy healing light;
Dispel the long night's lingering gloom,
And pierce the shadows of the tomb.

O come, thou Lord of David's Key!   15
The royal door fling wide and free;
Safeguard for us the heavenward road,
And bar the way to death's abode.

The titles in each first line refer to Jesus.

Franciscan processional hymn, French 15th century, tr. T. Lacey, in *The English Hymnal*, London, 1906

1.2 Preparation for death

Vanity of vanities, and all is vanity, except to love God and to serve Him only.
This is the highest wisdom, through contempt of the world to journey towards
Heaven ... Happy is he that daily prepares himself to die ... When it is morning,
think thou may not live till evening. When evening comes, dare not promise
thyself the morning ... Trust not on friends; neither put off thy salvation till   5
hereafter; men will forget thee sooner than thou thinkest. It is better to send
good works before thee than trust to other men's help ... Chastise thy body now
by penance, that thou mayest at death have confidence ... The patient man uses
violence to himself and labours to bring the flesh wholly into subjection to the
spirit ... Make now friends to thyself by venerating the Saints of God and   10
imitating their actions: that when thou failest in this life, they may receive thee
into everlasting habitations.

Written between 1418 and 1442, this collection of meditations was the most popular
devotional book of the 15th and 16th centuries.

**Thomas à Kempis, an Augustinian canon, *The Imitation of Christ*, ed.
C. Bigg, London, 1898, pp. 46, 86–8, 90**

1.3   The good man on his deathbed

Originally written in about 1416, this extremely popular handbook went through 23 printed editions in eight languages before 1500. A friar offers a candle to the dying man. Saints and the crucified Christ (top right) offer hope of salvation. Devils (foreground) try to distract him and claim his soul, but are defeated. Angels (top left) receive his soul (the tiny naked figure).

From *The Art of Dying Well*, German, *c.* 1470 (British Museum)

Questions

1   Explain the meaning of:
    (a) 'exile' [**1.1 line 3**]
    (b) 'the quarry from the lion's claw' [**1.1 line 8**]
    (c) 'the royal door' [**1.1 line 16**]
    (d) 'send good works before thee' [**1.2 lines 6–7**]
    (e) 'vanity' [**1.2 line 1**]
2   Consider how pessimistic the tone of **1.1** is.
3   'The time for a coming is near. See to it that you are prepared' (Thomas
    à Kempis, *c*. 1430). How does **1.1** help us to understand the theme of
    1.2? Read pages 29–30 before you answer.
4   (a) What does **1.1** see as Jesus' role in the process of salvation?
    (b) What does **1.2** say is the role of the individual in that process?
5   **1.3** is a sermon in picture. Use **1.2** to write a brief sermon explaining
    how to become 'a good man on his deathbed'.
6   What would be the purpose of an image like **1.3**?

The sacraments and salvation

Salvation was the central theme of the pursuit of holiness and at its heart was
one question: how could sinful men and women be acceptable to God?
Admission to heaven had become possible through the suffering, death and
resurrection of Jesus. 'Without the voluntary and innocent death of Our
Lord, no satisfaction would have been rendered to divine justice for the
multiple sins of the human race' (Cardinal Nicholas of Cusa, 1440). But individuals still needed divine mercy and forgiveness, so the process of becoming acceptable, termed justification, was of vital importance; by definition,
only the justified could enter heaven. All agreed that 'grace' was the vital
requirement and that it was distributed by God, principally through the
church in its seven sacraments. But what was 'grace'? It was defined as a
power, a divine quality infused by God into individuals. It forgave sin,
cleansed the soul and created habits of good living; it made people holy. That
holiness, that cleansing was, however, always in jeopardy for further sin
undermined it. The pilgrimage of life would be a constant struggle to reduce
sinfulness. Individuals were encouraged, therefore, to live 'in imitation of
Christ in his virtue' (Cardinal d'Ailly, 1416) as their only hope of salvation.
And since everyone had continual need of 'the divine medicine' (St
Augustine, about AD 420), they must return over and over to its prime
source, the sacraments.

Table 1: Justification	
The problem	**The solution**
When divine law demands sin be punished, how can a sinner ever be acceptable to God? Since the Fall (the first sin of Adam and Eve) mankind has been inherently wicked, crippled by an inclination to sin ('original sin').	Divine law's demand that sin must be punished is totally satisfied by Jesus' self-sacrifice on the cross. Admission to heaven is now possible. Inherent inclination to sin ('concupiscence') remains, but can be overcome because individual sins will be forgiven and cleansing grace dispensed.

Chief among the sacraments – divinely instituted rituals – were the mass and penance. Both take us to the core of late medieval devotion. Mass commemorated the crucifixion, yet was far more than a memorial. Each mass was seen as being enriched with healing power to forgive sin and reconcile individuals to God. It did so because, by miracle, the bread and wine, while keeping their outward form, were transformed into the very body and blood of Christ. The potency of the mass was thus formidable: 'it invokes the sufferings of Our Lord and applies them to fallen man, bought at great price from the clutches of Satan, for healing and redemption. By it, He nourishes us from his wounded breast' (Cardinal Cajetan, 1509). When seeking forgiveness, worshippers were directed to look backwards in gratitude. When seeking help to avoid future sin, they were taught to look forwards in hope. And especially outside Italy, they were encouraged in the 15th century to feel personal guilt by linking their own sins to Christ's passion. They were themselves responsible for the crucifixion.

1.4 'Behold, the Man of Sorrows'

An arrow represents lust, an oaksprig and acorn the devil. A crescent moon and star on the head-dress of the figure, lower left, represents antichrist and probably reflects the strong anti-Semitism of that age. The upper two tormentors are dressed as mercenaries. Following Psalm 21 v. 17, the tormentors were often described as savage dogs; one of the devils in 1.3 is a dog. The lower right tormentor is a mad dwarf and deformity was taken as a sign of sinfulness.

Hieronymus Bosch, *Christ Mocked***, Flemish,** *c.* **1490–5 (National Gallery, London)**

1.5   The crucifixion as mass

The angels collecting blood are a direct reference to the mass. The kneeling figures are St Jerome (left) and St Mary Magdalene. Legend said Mary was a reformed prostitute. Jerome, bare chested with rock in hand, beat himself to stop sexual temptation. Both represent the redemptive power of the crucifixion and were popular models for the discipline of penance. Their presence reflects contemporary concern with morality (see 6.11–6.16). This was painted for the altar of an Italian church.

Raphael, *The Crucified Christ with Saints and Angels,* **Italian,** *c.* **1503 (National Gallery, London)**

1.6

The pointing figure (St John the Baptist) emphasises Christ's suffering and commands personal involvement by the viewer. He also stands in front of water which, given that it was John who baptised Jesus, refers to the restoring power of sacramental grace. The cross bends under the weight of human sin carried by Jesus. Lambs were traditional animals of sacrifice. Jesus called himself the 'Lamb of God'. Here, the lamb bleeds into a cup and thus symbolises mass. This was painted for the altar of an Alsatian hospital specialising in skin diseases and syphilis.

Matthias Grünewald, *The Crucifixion* from *The Isenheim Altarpiece*, German, *c*. 1513 (Unterlinden Museum, Colmar)

1.7   The purpose of religious images

[Images] were introduced for three reasons. *First*, on account of the ignorance of
simple people, so that those who are not able to read the scriptures can yet learn
by seeing the sacraments of our salvation and faith in pictures ... It is one thing
to adore a painting, but it is quite another to learn from a painted narrative what
to adore. What a book is to those who can read, a picture is to the ignorant   5
people who look at it. Because in a picture even the unlearned may see what
example they should follow ... *Second*, images were introduced on account of our
emotional sluggishness; so that men who are not aroused to devotion when they
hear about the histories of the Saints may at least be moved when they see them,
as if actually present, in pictures. For our feelings are aroused by things seen   10
more than by things heard. *Third*, they were introduced on account of our
unreliable memories ... Images were introduced because many people cannot
retain in their memories what they hear, but they do remember if they see.

**Michele da Carcano, a Dominican, 'On Adoration', a sermon published
in Venice, 1492, in M. Baxandall, *Painting and Experience in Fifteenth
Century Italy: A Primer in the Social History of Pictorial Style*, by
permission of Oxford University Press, 2nd edn, 1988, p. 41**

1.8   Directing the thoughts of the congregation during mass

Have meditation how our Lord, the Saviour of all mankind, most willingly
offered Himself to His eternal Father, to be the sacrifice and oblation for man's
redemption ... so every man and woman that is in grace both the living and the
dead may be refreshed by that blessed sacrament. For not only it reneweth and
feedeth by grace and augmentation of the same the souls of them that living do   5
duly honour it but also it is remission of pain an indulgence to all the souls that
be in purgatory ... Therefore with pure heart and contrite soul in all your whole
affection and love honour this blessed sacrament to the profit of your own soul,
your friends and all Christian souls, both quick and dead ... For like as bread and
wine be those things which most conveniently sustain and relieve the necessities   10
of the body, so our blessed Lord will give unto us, under the qualities and taste
of bread and wine, His blessed Body and Blood as most convenient and
wholesome food, to restore and relieve all the necessities of soul and body unto
everlasting glory.

**'Meditations in the Time of Mass', French, *c.* 1480, in G. Dix, *The Shape
of the Liturgy*, Dacre Press, London, 1945, pp. 605–7**

1.9 Emotion and enthusiasm – anarchic religion or conditioned response?

1.9(a)

The better to impress the story of the Passion on your mind, and to
memorise each action of it more easily, it is helpful and necessary to fix the
places and people in your mind: a city, for example, which will be the city of
Jerusalem – taking for this purpose a city that is well known to you. In this city
find the principal places in which all the episodes of the Passion would have   5
taken place ... And then too you must shape in your mind some people, people
well-known to you, to represent for you the people involved in the Passion ...
When you have done all this, putting all your imagination into it, then go into
your chamber. Alone and solitary, excluding every external thought from your
mind, start thinking of the beginning of the Passion, starting with how Jesus   10
entered Jerusalem on the ass. Moving slowly from episode to episode, meditate
on each one, dwelling on each single stage and step of the story. And if at any
point you feel a sensation of piety, stop: do not pass on as long as that sweet and
devout sentiment lasts.

The Garden of Prayer, **Venice, 1494, a devotional manual for adolescent
girls, in Baxandall,** *Painting and Experience,* **p. 46**

1.9(b)

She had so great mind of the Passion of Our Lord Jesu Christ and of His
precious wounds and how dearly He bought her, that she cried and roared
wonderfully, so that she might be heard a great way off, and might not restrain
herself therefrom. Then had she great wonder how Our Lady might suffer or
endure to see His precious body be scourged and hanged on the cross. Also it   5
came to her mind how men had said to her before, that Our Lady, Christ's own
Mother, cried not as she did, and that caused her to say in her crying, 'Lord, I
am not Thy Mother. Take away this pain from me, for I may not bear it. Thy
passion will slay me' ...
    She came into a fair church, where she beheld a crucifix that was piteously   10
devised and lamentable to behold, through beholding which the Passion of Our
Lord entered her mind, whereby she began to melt and dissolve utterly in tears
of pity and compassion. Then the fire of love kindled so quickly in her heart that
she might not keep it privy ... as though she had seen Our Lord with her bodily
eye suffering His Passion at that time. Before her in her soul she saw Him verily   15
by contemplation and that caused her to have compassion.

Margery was the illiterate wife of a mayor of King's Lynn who dictated her book between
about 1432 and 1436.

The Book of Margery Kemp, **ed. S. B. Meech and H. E. Allen, The Council
of the Early English Text Society, CCXII, 1940, pp. 164, 111, 68**

Questions

1 (a) What was the official role of images [1.7]?
   (b) Why should images have an official role?
   (c) Comment on the estimate of the capabilities of the laity in **1.7**.
2 'Christ's stare into our eyes [1.4] is unsettling, almost accusative' (Smith, *Early Netherlandish and German Paintings*, 1985).
   (a) Comment on the symbolism in this picture.
   (b) Why was Jesus portrayed in this way?
3 (a) Explain why both **1.6** and **1.7** make explicit reference to mass.
   (b) How do you account for the radically different images of the crucifixion in **1.6** and **1.7**? In your answer, consider the variations in background and the atmosphere of each picture, as well as the characterisation of Jesus and the other figures.
4 Use **1.8** and the table on page 11 to explain how **1.6** and **1.7** offer fulfilment of the plea in **1.1**.
5 (a) Why does **1.9(a)** encourage the use of simple, familiar imagery?
   (b) Does **1.9(b)** show that Margery used a similar technique?
   (c) 'These manifestations of popular piety, the very things that Protestants would attack, were to a devout person like Margery not a hindrance but a direct help and stimulus to more spiritual devotion' (Pantin, *The English Church in the Fourteenth Century*, 1955). Comment.

Penance

From 1215, Catholics had been required to confess their sins to their priest at least once a year. This was the sacrament of penance, the great medieval instrument of justification. Its rituals mixed discipline with consolation and hope. In the 15th century priests increasingly counselled and guided, examined consciences and used guilt to reform behaviour. The emphasis was shifting more and more to the pastoral rather than the disciplinary – hence novel encouragements to confess as frequently as once a month or confession for children aged over seven. Above all, penance was where sins were forgiven, grace distributed and justification obtained. 'Peccavi, Domine, miserere mei' (Lord I have sinned. Have mercy upon me) was the soul-saving phrase everyone was taught. In penance, salvation was made tangible.

Table 2: Justification – medieval dispute

The problem

Do people have to do anything to be justified? Can they prepare themselves, co-operate in the process, even initiate it? The two basic schools of thought differed primarily over:
(a) the relationship between God's gifts of grace and free will;
(b) the state of mankind after the Fall.
It is vital to remember that shades of opinion between these extremes were many and common.

The schola antiqua	The schola Augustiniana
St Thomas Aquinas (d. 1274) taught that concupiscence is not all-dominating. Something of the original perfect humanity survives so people are themselves able to see God and want to obey him. God responds to that wish with an initial gift of grace.	St Augustine (d. 430) taught a pessimistic view of post-Fall humanity. Concupiscence is so strong that nobody is able even to recognise God, let alone want to do good. Free will has been lost. We are slaves to sin.
The initiative thus lies with mankind. Human effort is flawed by sin, but the crucifixion has cancelled the debt of punishment so God chooses to accept and reward it.	Individuals are thus totally dependent on God for their salvation. It is God who decides whether or not to choose them and it is God who stimulates genuine regret for sin. Justification is gratuitous and unmerited, given by God because of the merit earned by Christ on the cross.
Justification is now a gradual, lifelong process of adding healing grace and reducing concupiscence, both fruits of the sacraments.	Justification is thus an instantaneous process. Afterwards, concupiscence will be reduced by the grace of the sacraments so that the justified can co-operate with God. But salvation is not involved for it is already assured.

Precisely how justification worked became the subject of major 15th-century theological debate. Once, such a lack of defined position on so crucial a subject was taken to demonstrate the confusion symptomatic of an institution in decay. Now, such diversity is seen as indicating the exact opposite and the opportunity is taken to stress how such variations co-existed happily. They might argue over how something worked but not about whether it worked. Most late medieval theologians held that individuals could co-operate with God in their own salvation. A growing minority, however, claimed that humanity was so inherently wicked that justification could only be God's work.

The minority view, based on the teachings of St Augustine, serves as an important corrective. Beyond reminding us of the variety within medieval religion, it emphasises that not all tried to ascend a 'ladder of perfection'. Medieval Catholicism possessed a powerful 'theology of the cross', offering a personal conversion experience and salvation through the grace of Christ alone. Here there was no need to search for merit, for God had descended to us. While we should not underestimate the influence of powerful preachers in the Augustinian cause, few were capable of following the academic debate. The majority opinion is the one that needs primarily to concern us. It has been suggested that 'association between effort and salvation imposed a psychological burden' (Ozment, 1980), driving our late medieval ancestors along a frenzied quest for certainty of salvation through greater and greater effort. The 'burden' thesis has, however, found little scholarly support, its examples being based on extreme, atypical confessors' manuals and its entire proposition undermined by Protestant criticism which unanimously argued confessors were far too lenient. Another intriguing suggestion, that late medieval anticlericalism was fuelled 'not so much by clerical incompetence and corruption as the growing clerical efficiency and control penance made possible' (Tentler, 1974), remains an unproven hypothesis.

1.10   Confession: varieties of approach

1.10(a)

Let the priest be cautious and discreet, so that, like a skilled physician, he may pour wine and oil on the wounds of the injured man, diligently examining the circumstances of both sin and sinner, through which he may prudently learn what kind of advice he should offer, and what kind of remedy he should apply – trying various methods – to heal the sick man.

1.10(b)

But when it has finally come so far that one is sufficiently pure, that is that one has a clear conscience so that one no longer ... looks at God as a judge who metes out punishment, but as the completely desirable, and lovable ... then fly with a feeling of security into the arms of Christ, embrace him and kiss him.

1.10(c)

Beware a presumptuous confidence in God's mercy for no one is saved by his own righteousness, but only by divine mercy ... Already you can see how appropriate it is that the tax collectors and prostitutes precede us into the kingdom of heaven ... It follows, therefore, that those have nothing in common with Christ who do not participate with Him in sin, who claim righteousness for   5
themselves, who spurn sinners. After all, this love is the highest mercy, which falls immediately upon the deepest misery, concerned as it is before anything else with the extinction of sin.

1.10(a) *Omnis utriusque,* papal bull of 1215; 1.10(b) Jean Gerson, Chancellor of the University of Paris, *On Mystical Theology,* 1407; 1.10(c) Johann von Staupitz, vicar-general of the German Observant Augustinians, *Eternal Predestination,* Nuremberg, 1517. All extracts in *The Pursuit of Holiness in Late Medieval and Renaissance Religion,* ed. C. Trinkaus and H. Oberman, E. J. Brill, Leiden, 1974, pp. 104, 20, 21

1.11 Blessed assurance: the Augustinian solution

[The priest at confession] began to reason with me that the way of salvation was much broader than many persuaded themselves ... After I had left him, I began to think over for myself what that salvation is, and what our condition is. And I understood truly that if I did all the penances possible, and even many more, they would not be enough at one great stroke, I shall not say to merit that   5
salvation, but to atone for my past sins ... As regards the satisfaction for the sins committed, and into which human weakness falls, His passion is sufficient and more than sufficient. Through this thought I was changed from great fear and suffering to happiness ... I asked Him to let me share in the satisfaction which He, without any sins of His own, had made for us. He was quick to accept me   10
and to cause the Father completely to cancel the debt I had contracted, which I by myself was incapable of satisfying.

Gasparo Contarini, a Venetian noble, April 1511, in H. Jedin, 'Contarini und Camaldoli', *Archivo italiano per la storia della pietà,* II, 1959, p. 64†

Questions

1 (a) Why should penance be described in medical terms [1.10(a)]?
   (b) Do you think it worked for the benefit of the people? Explain your answer.

2   From the table on page 18 explain how the *schola antiqua* and *schola Augustiniana* differed over:
    (i)   concupiscence
    (ii) the role of the individual and human merit
    (iii) the role of the sacraments in justification
3   Summarise Contarini's theological position [**1.11**].
4   (a) Explain how you can tell from **1.10(b)** and **1.10(c)** where their authors stood in the debate on justification.
    (b) Assess the positions of **1.2**, **1.5** and **1.6** in this controversy.
5   Why do historians need to recognise the variety and diversity in late medieval Catholicism?

Flagellants

It seems impossible to say how popular penance was. Historians have to balance the obvious therapy it offered (think no further than the demand in our own day for psychoanalysis) with the requirement for self-accusation. Some at least 'came by all accounts in an aggressive and self-righteous mood' (Bossy, 1985). But come they did, whether out of fear of the exclusion from communion and community that would follow if they did not or, ultimately, out of fear of the final judgement. We face the greatest of problems for historians: analysing motivation. One penance which is particularly difficult to explicate is flagellation. An ancient ascetic tradition within Christianity stressed struggle with the self to achieve holiness; both body and will must be tamed. Penitential practices such as sleeping on the floor, wearing hairshirts or no shoes were everyday practices. Many went further and, by wearing a chain with spikes or walking with sharp stones in their shoes, inflicted on themselves physical pain. The flagellants must be seen within that tradition and, by the values of their day, their actions were entirely normal. Although it had originally been a phenomenon of the mid-13th century, the catastrophe of the Black Death one hundred years later was responsible for lay flagellation entering mainstream Catholicism. Thereafter, its popularity fluctuated unpredictably. Rarely was it imposed by a priest at confession. Rather, it was a voluntary penance, an exercise in empathetic devotion to the sufferings of Christ in his passion. In the public mind, however, it was most firmly linked with disaster, the hand of God. Individually and collectively in companies, flagellants appeared on the streets in time of plague trying to appease God's wrath and thereby forestall divine punishment, of themselves and their community. As the half millennium approached and voices began to cry that the end was nigh, few public religious ceremonies were without their companies of flagellants an apparent example of corporate devotion to achieve communal survival. Tempting as such a view seems, the blunt fact is that organised public flagellation was less prominent and extravagant in 1500 than it had been in 1400. Its prime appeal, as in all other penances, was as a medicine for one's own soul: 'It provided immediate and violent relief from guilt. In the very process, participants could feel that they were washing away their own sins' (Henderson, 1978).

1.12   Flagellants and devotion

1.12(a)

The penitent man kneels before an altar, on which is a casket containing holy relics.

Albrecht Dürer, *The Flagellant*, German, 1510 (Courtauld Art Gallery, London)

1.12(b)

I am unable to describe the devotion and piety shown by the crowds or to relate
the public repentance and humility to be seen all around, what beating of breasts,
what anguish in everyone's faces, what crying, what pain and anguish they
showed raising their hands to Heaven as they begged for pardon. They beat
themselves over and over, inflicting great pain, for they knew that their very sins   5
had inflicted terrible wounds on the Christ they saw before them, and now they
wished to wash away their guilt with tears and to purge the stains of sin with
pain. I tell you truly, from those groans and sighs, from those bruises and tears
there emerged such sweet consolation, happiness, celebration.

Francesco Ariosto, a lawyer, describing the ceremony exhibiting a major relic in Rome in
1471.

F. Ariosto, *Dicta de la entrata in Roma de lo illustrissimo duca Borso*, ed. E.
Celani, *Archivo della Società Romana di Storia Patria*, **XIII**, 1890, pp. 434–5†

Indulgences

One noticeable feature of the practice of late medieval religion is 'an arith-
metic of salvation' (Iserloh, 1961). Quantity was what seemed to matter. The
more penances performed, the more masses celebrated, the greater the spiritual benefit. The sacraments were becoming an automatic grace-dispensing
machine kept permanently running. Nothing illustrates that description
better than the use of indulgences – a primary method by which the late
medieval church helped the laity in their quest for justification and a prime
example of the way the disciplinary road was lightened for the faithful; no
burden here. Indulgences were not a sacrament. Rather they were a 'privilege', an extra source of grace. They drew their power from the belief that
Jesus' self-sacrifice on the cross had more than compensated for all the sins
of every generation, leaving an equally vast surplus of his goodness ('merit')
unconsumed. Sometimes called a 'larder of grace', that surplus had been
entrusted to the church to distribute for the spiritual benefit of all Christians.
Catholic theology distinguished between the guilt incurred by a sin and the
penalty due for committing that sin. Through the sacraments, guilt could be
washed away, but such was their concept of justice as retribution ('forensic
justice') that punishment would still be due for every forgiven sin. That was
where indulgences came in. By transferring some of Christ's surplus merit,
the penalty could be remitted, if the penitent was truly repentant. That is
a key point, frequently misunderstood then as now. Indulgences did not

forgive sin. Neither were they a substitute for sacramental penance. Instead, they worked hand in hand with it.

While indulgences were available originally only to the living, medieval Catholicism's increasing concern for the dead virtually guaranteed pressure to extend provision beyond the grave. Church teaching was clear: the justified went straight to heaven, the unjustified to hell. But what of those who died with their sins forgiven (in a state of grace and thus justified), but with residual punishment still outstanding? As yet unfit for heaven, their souls needed cleansing in the purifying fires of purgatory, which thus completed the disciplinary work of penance. Such souls gradually came within the care of the church. From 1274, special masses to aid them were celebrated. From about 1355, Franciscans began offering indulgences to pilgrims at Assisi to help souls already in purgatory – although they had no official sanction for this practice. Finally, the Franciscan pope, Sixtus IV, conceded the long-cherished bull formally extending the operation of the treasury of merits to the dead. While we should not overlook the strength of 'social piety' toward family and friends reflected in medieval attitudes to death, these rites were primarily matters of religion, of the quest for holiness. Purgatory and indulgences were inseparable. In no other age did fear of the former and respect for the latter flourish as in the 15th century.

1.13   Indulgence theory

1.13(a)

[Jesus did not] redeem us with corruptible things – with silver and gold –
but with his own precious blood, which he is known to have poured out as an
innocent victim on the altar of the cross: not a mere measured drop of blood
(which however because of its union with the Word would have sufficed for the
redemption of all humanity), but as it were an unmeasured flood ...   5
    Now this treasure he entrusted to be dispensed for the weal of the faithful ...
through blessed Peter, who bore the keys of heaven, and Peter's successors as
God's own representatives on earth. The purposes served should be proper and
reasonable: sometimes total, sometimes partial remission of punishment due for
temporal sins ... and for those ends the treasure should be applied in mercy to   10
those who are truly penitent and have made their confession.

Unigenitus, **bull of Clement VI, January 1343**

1.13(b)

That the salvation of souls may be secured above all at that time when they most
need the intercession of others and are least able to help themselves, we wish by
our Apostolic authority to draw on the treasury of the Church and to succour the
souls in purgatory who died united in Christ through love and whose lives have
merited that such intercession should now be offered through an Indulgence ... If   5
any parent, friend or other Christians are moved by piety towards these very
souls who are exposed to the fire of purgatory for the expiation of punishments
which by divine justice are their due: let them ... give a fixed amount or value of
money ... for the repair of the church[1] ... it is then our will that plenary remission
should avail by intercession for the said souls in purgatory, to win them relief   10
from their punishments.

[1] This grant was made for the repair of a church in France. Rapidly it was copied and
repeated in a wide variety of contexts.

Salvator Noster, **bull of Sixtus IV, August 1476. Both extracts in E. G.
Rupp and B. D. Drewery, *Martin Luther*, Edward Arnold, London, 1970,
pp. 13–14**

1.14   An indulgence preacher at work

Hear the cry of your dead parents, 'Have mercy on me, have mercy on me. Our
punishment is severe and we are in great pain. You could save us from these
agonies with a small payment, yet you do nothing ... We made you, fed you,
cared for you and left you our worldly goods. It will take only a little to release
us. Why are you so cruel, leaving us to lie here burning and boiling in the   5
flames?'

**Johann Tetzel, a Dominican, 'Sermon to the people of Zerbst' (1517), in
W. Köhler, *Dokumente zum Ablasstreit von 1517* (Tübingen, 1934), p. 126.†
Tetzel's extravagant indulgence preaching inflamed Luther to write the
95 Theses.**

Questions

1   (a)   Why according to **1.12b** was flagellation performed?
    (b)   Suggest reasons why the atmosphere in **1.12(a)** is so different to
          1.12(b).
    (c)   Must **1.2 lines 7–9** refer to flagellation? Explain your answer.
2   Explain the meaning of:
    (i)   'this treasure' [**1.13(a) line 6**]
    (ii) 'Peter's successors' [**1.13(a) line 7**]

   (iii) 'our Apostolic authority' **[1.13(b) line 3]**
   (iv) 'the expiation of punishments' **[1.13(b) line 7]**
3 (a)   How do the terms of qualification for indulgence differ from **1.13(a)** to **1.13(b)**?
  (b)   How do you account for those differences?
  (c)   Explain the attitude of **1.2** to the alternative types of indulgences.
  (d)   How could **1.8** see mass as an indulgence **[line 6]**?
4 Explain the connections between the bleeding lamb **[1.6]**, penance **[1.10 (a), (b) and (c)]** , indulgences and purgatory.
5 'Much of the impetus for the growth of the indulgence system came from below' (Ozment, *The Age of Reform*, 1980). Comment.

Summary

From the evidence of this chapter and from your wider reading, assess the validity of the following criticisms of late medieval religion:
  (i) 'Piety was sentimental because the people were ignorant. The clergy conditioned but did not teach them' (Lortz, *How the Reformation Came*, 1964)
 (ii) 'A mechanical performance of half-christianised rituals. A formal rather than a personal religion, rooted in fear and magic' (Toussaert, *Le Sentiment religieux en Flandre à la fin du moyen âge*, 1963)
(iii) 'The main failing of official piety was the absence of a distinctive concept of lay religious life and the consequent imposition of traditional clerical and monastic ideals upon a laity increasingly literate, urban, socially mobile and demanding respectful treatment' (Ozment, *The Age of Reform*, 1980)
(iv) 'The medieval church demanded too much, rather than too little. Its expectations and prescribed routines had made lay religion psychologically burdensome' (Cameron, *The European Reformation*, 1991)

References

L. Febvre, 'The Origins of the French Reformation: A Badly-Put Question?' Originally published in 1929 and now available in *A New Kind of History and Other Essays*, ed. P. Burke, Routledge, 1973
J. Henderson, 'The Flagellant Movement and Flagellant Confraternities', *Studies in Church History*, XV, 1978
E. Iserloh, 'Der Wert der Messe in der Diskussion der Theologen', *Zeitschrift für katholische Theologie*, LXXXIII, 1961
J. Lortz, *How the Reformation Came*, Herder and Herder, New York, 1964

H. Oberman, *Luther and the Dawn of the Modern Era*, Brill, Leiden, 1974

S. Ozment, *The Age of Reform*, Yale University Press, 1980

W. Pantin, *The English Church in the Fourteenth Century*, Cambridge University Press, 1955

A. Smith, *Early Netherlandish and German Paintings*, National Gallery, London, 1985

T. Tentler, 'The Summa for Confessors as an Instrument of Social Control', in *The Pursuit of Holiness in Late Medieval and Renaissance Religion*, ed. C. Trinkaus and H. Oberman, E. J. Brill, Leiden, 1974

K. Thomas, *Religion and the Decline of Magic*, Weidenfeld, 1971

J. Toussaert, *Le Sentiment religieux en Flandre à la fin du moyen âge*, Plon, Paris, 1963

For Bossy (1985) and Cameron, see *Suggestions for further reading*.

2 Internal reform 1480–1542

In this chapter we turn from beliefs to the institutional church. Traditionally, because the pre-Reformation century was deemed an era of spiritual recession, the pre-Reformation church was judged decadent, inefficient and unresponsive to the needs of clergy or people. Corruption led to Reformation. Modern scholarship has radically altered that perspective. Now, all would agree that 'the age was one of astonishing religious creativity' (Rice, 1970) and current historians judge the church's condition to have been 'reasonably healthy' (Chaunu, 1989), and 'moderately satisfying' (Cesareo, 1990). Further, most accept that the Reformation was a rebellion over theology, not abuses. Reform was high on the agenda throughout the 15th century and was under way well before Luther – hence the concept of 'Catholic Reformation' in current vogue. The need for reform in every institution is perennial; St Bernard of Clairvaux (d. 1153) condemned the church of his day as 'incurably degenerate'. But reform is an ambiguous concept. Reformist pressure could indicate that expectations and standards were rising. Calls for reform could provide evidence that the late medieval church was not only alive but adaptable, busily maintaining its relevance and membership in the fast-shifting sands of an era of unprecedented cultural, social, economic and political change. Our task is to establish what was on the reformers' agenda and to understand their ambitions.

The western church of 1500 was probably in better health than the church of St Bernard; it was certainly no worse. Who called for reform in 1500? Were complaints made by wreckers out to destroy the church, by agitators aiming to rejuvenate it or by sensationalists exploiting tales of scandal? Did the complaints come from a new, better-educated laity able to engage in a deeper piety but exasperated by the inadequacies of their clergy? Or were the complainants the clergy themselves? Was the church its own sternest critic? Were denunciations accurate or exaggerated? How far did they agree upon what needed to be done? Did they reject the doctrinal teachings of the church or did their criticisms relate to problems of internal church management: the need to improve administration and personnel? And were their aims revolutionary (trying to change to something new) or conservative (wanting to recover something lost)? The root of our problem is that, as Haller pointed out as long ago as 1903, reformist activity gives 'an excellent picture of the prevailing mood [but] a poor picture of prevailing conditions'.

The end of the world?

That late medieval mood was shaped by an accelerating sense of doom: the Last Judgement was imminent. The combination of contemporary disasters, the conviction that standards of behaviour were falling, the rising splendour of church art and the discovery of new lands across the ocean where Christianity could spread, together convinced many that the apocalypse was about to dawn. In the apocalypse, a final confrontation between good and evil would take place before Christ returned to judge mankind: 'The generation from 1480 was more censorious than any before' (Renaudet, 1958). They held to a decline-theory of history. The prophets said that the last age would be more sinful than any other. But some followed Abbot Joachim of Fiore (d. 1202) in believing biblical evidence showed that, after severe divine punishment, the last age would be purified. The apocalypse brought repentance and renewal, as well as judgement and punishment. Both viewpoints inevitably affected opinions as to the urgency of reform. Did they also so distort judgements that late medieval assessments of the church need to be treated with great caution? The danger is that, mesmerised by the search for lost purity, they talked down the actual situation and therefore themselves caused totally unnecessary damage to the church's reputation.

2.1 Apocalyptic alarm

[For twenty years I] expounded to nearly all of Italy John's Apocalypse[1] concerning the destiny of the Church, and repeatedly asserted that those who were then listening would see great agitation and destruction in the Church and would one day behold its correction.... [G] rant to me the power to speak, to my address the power to persuade, to the Fathers ... [of this] Council, to root out   5 vice, to arouse virtue, to catch the foxes who in this season swarm to destroy the holy vineyard.... [U] nless the sword is put down and we return again into the bosom of piety at the altars and shrines of God, [the infidel] will grow stronger day by day, will subjugate all to his power, and as the wicked avenger of our impiety will take possession of the entire world .... [U] nless by this Council ...   10 we place a limit on our morals, unless we force our greedy desire for human things, the source of evils, to yield to love of divine things, it is all over with

Christendom .... When has life been more effeminate? ... When has the license to sin been more shameless? ... When have the signs, portents, and prodigies both of a threatening heaven and of a terrified earth appeared more numerous or more horrible?   15

¹ The Book of Revelation.

Cardinal Giles of Viterbo, Prior-General of the Augustinian Friars, addressing the Vth Lateran Council, May 1512, in *Catholic Reform from Cardinal Ximenes to the Council of Trent, 1495–1563,* **ed. J. C. Olin, Fordham University Press, New York, 1990, pp. 48, 57–8**

Reform

Ideas on reform were as varied in scope and practicality as the reformers who proposed them. All, however, looked to the spreading ripples of individual example. The late medieval emphasis on confession and penance 'set norms of conduct into the conscience so that internal sanctions of guilt controlled behaviour' (Tentler, 1977). Until comprehensive, church-wide reform was ordered by the papacy or a general council, reform of and by the individual was the target; everyone had to do what they could. The next three sections look at areas of contemporary concern for reform: biblical scholarship, the clergy and the religious orders.

Reform by scholarship

Those most concerned with reform through biblical scholarship were the Christian Humanists, a disparate international brotherhood of scholars who rejected much contemporary religious practice as arid, most medieval theology as sterile, and looked to scholarship to restore right religion. Example and inspiration, they believed, lay in a lost golden age they located in the early church. The New Testament and the writings of the Fathers (the great theologians of the first five Christian centuries) were, they argued, full of refined wisdom and divine truths lost when the West abandoned Greek and Hebrew studies. These ancient texts, they believed, should be collected, printed and studied. The moral and spiritual regeneration of the present lay awaiting discovery in the past and the key to that past was textual criticism. Learning was to be the handmaid of religion. Knowledge would open the way to spiritual life. Not all were convinced. If textual revision was permitted, surely the credibility and authority of the church (whose teachings quoted the rejected Latin version) would be undermined? Even more controversial was the proposal to make these texts available to all. Vernacular Bibles before 1517 were not as rare as Luther would have us believe. Nonetheless, many clergy regarded them as inseparable from heresy. Did not the path to salvation lie in obedience? To open the Bible to textual scrutiny was dangerous enough. To open the Bible to popular scrutiny was to destroy the theologians' monopoly control of dogma – surely subversive. Theoretically that may have been so but the Christian Humanists were, almost without exception, emphatically not popularisers. They wrote in Latin or Greek, not for the mass market. Their whole ethos was elitist. It was Luther who made Bible-reading common, not Erasmus.

2.2 Ancient texts: the older the better

The more nearly a light approximates the intensity of the sun, the more brightly it shines ... The closer a thing is to its origin, the more purely it retains its own nature ... Writings which have come down to us from Apostolic times differ from others as living things differ from the dead ... [because] they preserve in themselves a living force and a marvellous light beyond all others.

Jacques Lefèvre d'Etaples, *Corpus Dionysiacum*, Paris, 1499, in E. F. Rice, 'The Humanist Idea of Christian Antiquity', *Studies in the Renaissance*, IX, Renaissance Society of America, New York, 1962, p. 136

2.3 Corrupt Latin rejected

There are many reasons ... that impel us to print the languages of the original text .... Words have their own character, and no translation ..., however complete, can entirely express their full meaning .... Scripture in translation inevitably remains ... laden with ... sublime truths which cannot be understood ....
[W] herever there is diversity in the Latin manuscripts or the suspicion of a   5
corrupted reading (... how frequently this occurs because of the ignorance and negligence of copyists), it is necessary to go back to the original source of Scripture .... [T] hat every student ... might have ... the original texts ... and be able to quench his thirst at the very fountainhead of the water that flows unto life everlasting ..., we ordered the original languages ... their translations adjoined,   10
to be printed ... [using] the most accurate and oldest manuscripts for our base texts.

Cardinal Ximenes, an Observant Franciscan and Archbishop of Toledo, Prologue to the *Complutensian Bible*, Alcala, begun 1502, published 1522, in Olin, *Catholic Reform*, pp. 62–4

2.4   Bibles for all

2.4(a)

I disagree very much with those who are unwilling that Scripture, translated into the vulgar tongue, be read by the uneducated, as if Christ taught intricate doctrines or the strength of the Christian religion consisted in men's ignorance of it ... I would that even the lowliest woman read the Gospels and Epistles. I would they were translated into all languages so that they could be read and   5
understood not only by Scots and Irish, but also by Turks and Saracens ... Would that, as a result, the farmer sing some portion of them at the plough, the weaver hum parts of them to the movement of his shuttle.

Erasmus, *Paraclesis* (preface) to his New Testament, Basle, 1516, in *Collected Works of Erasmus*, trs. R. A. Mynors and D. F. Thomson, University of Toronto Press Incorporated, 1982, 19, pp. 96–7

2.4(b)

For the praise and honour of God, the Blessed Virgin and all the saints, the Gospels read every Sunday at Mass are translated into Danish for the salvation of the people who, unable to understand Latin, cannot read how to live by God's commandments ... If the Evangelists were writing today for the people of Denmark, they would certainly write their Gospels in good Danish so that all   5
could understand. All people should know the Gospels in their own language.

Christian Pedersen, canon of Lund Cathedral, *Sunday Commentary*, 1515, in C. Brandt and R. Fenger, *Christian Pedersen Danske Skrifter*, Copenhagen, 1850, I, pp. xiii–xiv†

Questions

1   (a)   What needed reformation, according to **2.1**?
    (b)   Is **2.1** what you expected to find as an agenda for church reform? Explain your answer.
    (c)   Must we take Giles' analysis at face value [**2.1**]?
2   How does **2.2** help explain the demand in **2.3** for original texts?
3   Explain Erasmus' objective in **2.4(a)**.
4   Consider whether **2.4(a)** and **2.4(b)** are at odds with the aim of **2.3**.
5   'Let us both, my Erasmus, succour the faith in its infirmity' (Cardinal Sadoleto, 1528). From **2.2–2.4** and your wider reading, assess the strengths and limitations of Christian Humanist reform.

Reform of the clergy

Not a few reformers considered that the urgent need was for a transformation in the quality and commitment of the clergy. The church of 1500 struggled with the same problems as the church of 1100. The will to reform was unmistakably present. More than a few, bishops and priests alike, were keenly aware that all was far from well with their brother clerics. But how far were solutions within the church's competence? Where could be found tens of thousands of well-educated men of strong personal holiness eager for service in remote, poorly paid parishes? Complaints reveal that the fundamental problem was neither corruption nor immorality; they were but symptoms. The root cause was a lack of vocation for the priestly office; commitment to the spiritual and moral welfare of a congregation was rare. The clergy were lukewarm. They were not pastors. Why? The Middle Ages looked on church posts in material terms as instruments of power and privilege, to be manipulated to personal advantage; as pieces of property to be exploited. A career in the church was a good way to serve family interests or to gain political power. No medieval century envisaged bishops as the ideal civil servants, diplomats and ministers more than the 15th. Further, that century pushed aside earlier ambivalence to clerical wealth and positively 'celebrated the riches of church and clergy' (Baron, 1937). How could the church counter such a world view? It could not even choose a large proportion of its personnel. Parish priests were selected by the patron of the benefice – often universities or noblemen. As for the episcopate (and many of the senior clergy), by 1500 most outside Italy were pawns in a political game, selected by their kings rather than the pope in order to buy or reward service, to repay debts, to build or bolster favour. Patronage, not spirituality, determined promotion. As the Venetian ambassador to France noted in 1524, 'they deal in bishoprics and abbeys at court as elsewhere in pepper and cinnamon'.

2.5 Cardinals: stewards rather than lords

The cardinals might consider how they are the successors of the apostles ... and that they are not the lords but the stewards of the spiritual riches for every penny of which they will have to render an exact account ... And what need have they of wealth at all if they take the place of the apostles who were poor men?

They believe they do quite enough for Christ if they play their part as overseer by means of every kind of ritual, near-theatrical ceremonial and display, benedictions and anathemas, and all their titles of Your Beatitude, Reverence, and Holiness. For them ... teaching the people is too like hard work, interpreting the holy scriptures is for schoolmen, and praying is a waste of time; to shed tears is

5

weak and womanish, to be needy is degrading; to suffer defeat is a disgrace and   10
hardly fitting for one who scarcely permits the greatest of kings to kiss the toes of
his sacred feet.

**Erasmus, *Praise of Folly*, 1509, tr. B. Radice, reproduced by permission of
Penguin Books Ltd, Harmondsworth, 1971, pp. 177–80**

2.6   Advice to a new cardinal

We must esteem ourselves highly favoured for the many honours bestowed on
our house, but more particularly for having conferred on us, in your person, the
greatest dignity we have ever enjoyed ... Be grateful to God. Continually recollect
it is not through your merits this event has taken place. Repay His favour with a
pious, chaste and exemplary life ... It gave me great pleasure to learn that during   5
the last year you had frequently, of your own accord, gone to communion and
confession ... Now you are to reside at Rome, that sink of all iniquity, difficulty
of conducting yourself will increase. You will probably meet with those who will
endeavour to corrupt and incite you to vice. These oppose with the greatest
firmness, as there is at present less virtue amongst your brethren of the College   10
... You are now devoted to God and the Church; on which account aim at being
a good ecclesiastic. But it will not be difficult for you to favour your family and
your native place. You should be the link to bind our Florence closer to the
church, and our family with the city.

**Lorenzo to his son, Giovanni de Medici, 1490, in W. Roscoe, *The Life of
Lorenzo de Medici*, London, 1851, pp. 285–7**

2.7   Bishops as pastors

2.7(a)

Look not to authority over others. As the responsibility of the episcopal office is
extremely heavy, bishops have been appointed by Our Lord to feed and direct
the sheep, not to rule or dominate over them ... A bishop must be without
personal ambition, rejecting the values and riches of the world. Rather he must
commit himself to a life of self-sacrifice, of humility and service for he is to be a   5
physician of the soul. Therefore he must live a life of austerity and simplicity so
that he may be a vessel of the divine fire ... He must weep over the sins of his
flock. He must feel for his sheep and bring them to repentance by love, by
gentleness and by personal example. He must be the imitation of Christ, being
neither as princes nor as lords, but as fathers guided by mildness and charity ...   10
Our Lord stands patiently at the door of the soul and knocks gently. If that is the
way of the great Pastor, how can the way of the bishop be anything else?

**Lorenzo Giustiniani, Patriarch of Venice, *De Institutione et Regimine
Praelatorum*, written *c.* 1452, in *Opera Omnia*, Venice, 1751, caps. I–III, ix†**

2.7(b)

Your Grace, we doubt not the sorrowful decay of this land, as well in good Christianity as in laudable manners, has grown for lack of good prelates. Wherefore your Grace may do meritoriously to see such persons promoted to bishoprics, that their manner of living be examples of goodness and virtue. The residence of such shall do more good here than we can express.

Hugh Inge, a Dominican and Archbishop of Dublin to Cardinal Wolsey, February 1528, in *State Papers of Henry VIII*, **London, 1830, II, pp. 126–7**

2.8   Clerical standards: reform by legislation

2.8(a)

That clerics may live chastely and continently as required by the sacred canons, we decree that those who do the contrary be severely punished ... Toleration by superiors, contrary custom or other subterfuge cannot be accepted as justifiable excuses; these must be corrected and those who tolerate them punished in accordance with the law.

2.8(b)

That the nefarious pest simony be for ever banished from the Roman Curia and all Christendom, we hereby renew the constitutions published by our predecessors against it, decreeing their strict observance and the imposition of the penalties prescribed therein.

2.8(c)

That no clerics, whether seculars or members of any of the mendicant orders or any other order to which the office of preaching pertains by right, custom, privilege, or otherwise, be admitted to exercise that office unless they have first been carefully examined by their respective superiors and found competent and fit as regards moral integrity, age, knowledge, uprightness, prudence and exemplary life.

5

Decrees of the Vth Lateran Council (1512–17), in H. J. Schroeder, *Disciplinary Decrees of the General Councils*, **TAN Books and Publishers Inc., Illinois, 1937, pp. 496–7, 505**

2.9   Royal patronage

2.9(a)

We feel this to be a great injury[1] on the part of the pope, seeing that all we are asking for is just and reasonable, and that he denies us everything as though it

were unjust, and that His Holiness has so little respect for us and for the great
affection we have for him, and our desire to do things for him and the Apostolic
See ... we do not know what more a pope can do to offend us and show himself   5
our adversary, than provide to the churches of our kingdom without our petition,
undermining our royal powers of patronage, which are enforced in the most
minor kingdoms of the world, and refusing to do what we have asked in order to
protect the public weal of our kingdoms. If, for this, we want to do what all other
kings do, the remedy is in our hands, and we have very little need of what we   10
have asked His Holiness for.

¹ Rome had just rejected Ferdinand's nominee for the bishopric of Mdina (Malta).

**King Ferdinand of Aragon to Julius II, April 1504, in C. Shaw, *Julius II,
the Warrior Pope*, Basil Blackwell Publishers Ltd, Oxford, 1993, p. 221**

2.9(b)

When any cathedral or metropolitan church in that kingdom shall become vacant
... the King of France shall, within six months of that vacancy occurring, present
and nominate to Us and Our successors as Bishops of Rome a sober master or
graduate in theology or the laws, aged at least twenty-seven and in all other ways
suitable. That person nominated shall then be provided by Us. Should the King   5
fail to nominate a candidate properly qualified, the Holy See shall not be obliged
to invest that person and within three months the King shall nominate another.
Should the King fail in that duty, or should his second candidate also be
unqualified, We and Our successors shall be at liberty ourselves to provide a
suitably qualified person. Further, the Holy See shall always hold the right to   10
provide, without royal nomination, where vacancy occurs through death at the
Court of Rome.

**The Concordat of Bologna (Leo X to Francis I), January 1516, in
Ordonnances des rois de France: règne de François Ier, Paris, 1902, I,
pp. 442–3†**

Questions

1   Does **2.6** show primary concern for family or religion? Explain your
    answer.
2   Explain why bishops should be seen as the key to reform [**2.7(b)**].
3   (a)   How far are **2.5** and **2.7(a)** in agreement on the ideal senior church-
          man?
    (b)   What ideal do they propose?

4   From **2.8**, explain the meaning of:
   (i) 'simony' [**2.8(b) line 1**]
   (ii) 'seculars' [**2.8(c) line 1**]
   (iii) 'mendicant' [**2.8(c) line 1**]

5   What do the references in **2.8(a)** and **2.8(b)** to canons and constitutions tell us about the nature of the church's problems?

6   'Reform by legislation was the approach of the disciplinarian. Reform by love was the approach of the pastor. Between them existed a powerful tension' (Green, 'Reformed Pastors and *Bons Curés*', 1989). Discuss this proposition with reference to **2.5–2.8** and your wider reading.

7   (a)   Explain Ferdinand's final sentence in **2.9(a)**.
   (b)   Of what does he complain in the letter?

8   (a)   Find out why Leo granted the Concordat.
   (b)   Had Leo surrendered control of the French church? Justify your answer.

9   Consider how far the procedures and assumptions represented by **2.9(a)** and **2.9(b)** served or hindered church reform.

A new type of monasticism

A certain disenchantment with the monastic ideal pervaded the 15th century: 'Prevailing opinion thought there should be fewer religious rather than more' (Scarisbrick, 1988). Despite or perhaps because of that, all religious orders experienced reorganisation and some revitalisation. The pursuit of holiness through abstinence and discipline could still attract. Moves to recover a literal observance of the ancient Rule of an order in a life of prayer, strict poverty, austerity and humility were made too frequently to be dismissed as aberrations. Alone, such efforts were unlikely to save the day. In earlier crises, the monastic ideal had survived because it proved adaptable. Early monastic reform had tried to escape the world in remote places. Later movements embraced the world and moved into the bustle of urban life.

The way forward was pioneered in Italy. Out of the Oratories of the Divine Love – small urban religious societies established from 1494 at Franciscan inspiration – blossomed small groups like the Theatines (1524), the Barnabites (1530) and the Somaschi (1532). The largest and most influential, however, emerged from Spain: the Society of Jesus, founded by St Ignatius Loyola. Like the friars, these new orders took spirituality outside the cloister to work among clergy and people. But they were crucially different from all earlier foundations. They were versatile communities of 'clerks regular', working priests, not contemplative monks. What the world needed was the sacramental and pastoral ministry of the priesthood, organised with the discipline of an order: 'from the beginning, the Jesuits were primarily a company of pastors whose principal objective was the salvation of souls' (O'Malley, 1993). Ignatius' concept of that ministry marked them out in another fundamental way for they possessed an intense charitable concern, conceived on a wholly new scale. It is known as 'activism in grace' and was explained by the Theatine, Lorenzo Scupoli, as 'the active, purposeful struggle of the human will, fortified by Divine Grace, against sin and on behalf of the good of others'. Charity and piety were more than complementary. The care of the sick or poor was an act of devotion. Consciously or not, the new orders were founded within the spirit of contemporary criticism and Catholicism rapidly became inconceivable without them: 'Here was the individualism of the age taking its appropriate form in Catholic spirituality' (Evennett, 1968).

2.10 Jesuit beginnings: St Ignatius' conversion

Up to his twenty-sixth year he was a man given over to the vanities of the world, and took a special delight in the exercise of arms, with a great and vain desire of winning glory ... [Wounded in the war with France, 1521] he was not able to stand upon his leg, and so had to remain in bed. He had been much given to reading worldly books of fiction and knight errantry, and feeling well enough to   5
read he asked for some of these books to help while away the time. In that house, however, they could find none of those he was accustomed to read, and so they gave him a life of Christ and a book of the lives of the saints in Spanish. By the frequent reading of these books he conceived some affection for what he found there narrated. Pausing in his reading, he gave himself up to thinking over what   10
he had read. At other times he dwelt on the things of the world which formerly had occupied his thoughts ... In reading the life of our Lord and the lives of the saints, he paused to think and reason with himself, 'Suppose that I should do what St Francis did, what St Dominic did' ...
He determined, therefore, on a watch of arms throughout a whole night,   15
without ever sitting or lying down, but standing a while and then kneeling before the altar of our Lady at Montserrat,[1] where he had made up his mind to leave his fine attire and to clothe himself with the armour of Christ. Leaving, then, his place, he continued, as was his wont, thinking about his resolutions, and when he arrived at Montserrat [1522], after praying for a while and making an engagement   20
with his confessor, he made a general confession in writing which lasted three

days ... [In 1534, after studying at university, he and six companions came to a decision as to what they were going to do.] Their plan was to go to Venice and from there to Jerusalem, where they were to spend the rest of their lives for the good of souls. If they were refused permission to remain in Jerusalem they would   25
return to Rome, offer themselves to the Vicar of Christ, asking him to make use of them wherever he thought it would be more to God's glory and the good of souls.

[1] A famous Marian shrine in the Catalan abbey of Montserrat.

The autobiography was dictated between 1553 and 1555.

St Ignatius' Own Story, **ed. W. J. Young, Loyola University Press, Chicago, 1956, pp. 7–9, 15, 58**

2.11   Jesuit beginnings: original principles

... a community founded principally for the advancement of souls in Christian life and doctrine ... for the propagation of the faith by the ministry of the word, by spiritual exercises, by works of charity, and expressly by the instruction in Christianity of children and the uneducated .... [T] his entire society and each one individually are soldiers of God under faithful obedience to our most holy   5
lord Paul III and his successors and are thus under the command of the Vicar of Christ and his divine power not only as having the obligation to him which is common to all clerics, but also as being bound by the bond of a vow that whatever His holiness commands pertaining to the advancement of souls and the propagation of the faith we must immediately carry out, ... whether he sends us   10
to the Turks or to the New World or to the Lutherans or to others.

    All the companions who are in holy orders ... shall be bound to say the office according to the rites of the Church, but not in choir[1] lest they be led away from the works of charity to which we have all dedicated ourselves ... since as a consequence of the nature of our vocation, besides other necessary duties, we   15
must frequently be occupied a great part of the day and even of the night in comforting the sick both in body and in spirit.

[1] Choir offices were the heart of communal life to monastic orders.

Paul III approved this statement in September 1539 and the bull instituting the Jesuits (*Regimini militantis ecclesiae*) was issued in September 1540.

St Ignatius, *Prima Summa*, 1539, in Olin, *Catholic Reform*, pp. 83–4, 86

2.12   Special obedience: the fourth vow

2.12(a)

All of us who are mutually bound together in this Society have pledged ourselves
to the supreme pontiff, seeing that he is the lord of the entire harvest of Christ.
In this offering we have indicated to him that we are prepared for all that he may
in Christ decide in our case .... The reason that we subjected ourselves in this
way to his judgment and will was that we know that he has a greater knowledge   5
of what is advantageous to the whole of Christendom.

**Pierre Favre, a founder Jesuit, to Diego de Gouvea, November 1538, in
Olin,** *Catholic Reform,* **p. 81**

2.12(b)

They know the goal set before them: to procure the salvation and perfection of all
men and women. They understand that they are to that end bound by that
Fourth Vow to the supreme pontiff: that they might go on these universal
missions for the good of souls by his command ... They realise that they cannot
build or acquire enough houses to be able from nearby to run out to the combat.   5
Since this is the case, they consider that they are in their most peaceful and
pleasant house when they are constantly on the move, when they travel through
the earth.

**Jeronimo Nadal, a Jesuit and key member of the inner circle around St
Ignatius,** *Commentary on the Jesuit Constitutions,* **1561, in J. W. O'Malley,**
The First Jesuits, **Harvard University Press, Cambridge, Massachusetts,
1993, p. 301**

2.13   Activism in grace

The hospitals were ignored. Nobody made any effort to find out what was
happening or to organise any relief of the suffering. Piety and compassion had
fled ... The companions took action, as far as they were able, to relieve the great
need. They begged money in the streets and collected donations, both in cash
and in food, from house to house. They then searched the streets to find the   5
poor and starving and brought them back to the house. There they washed them
and gave them new clothes. They gave them medicine and food and taught some
catechism ... Sometimes there were as many as 300 crowded into the house
receiving comfort and spiritual guidance. In addition, the companions went out
daily to assist the two thousand starving and shivering in the streets of Rome's   10
poorest quarters, giving them food and money. The companions themselves
owned nothing, but Our Lord touched the hearts of good Romans who daily
brought gifts of money and clothing and medicines for this holy work.

From an account of Rome, 1538, in P. Tacchi-Venturi, *Storia della
Compagnia di Gesù in Italia,* **Rome, 1951, II, p. 163†**

Questions

1 Explain the meaning of:
  (i) 'knight errantry' [**2.10 line 5**]
  (ii) 'the entire harvest of Christ' [**2.12(a) line 2**]
2 What was the purpose of the 'watch at Montserrat' [**2.10**]?
3 Explain from **2.10–2.13** why Ignatius forbade communal choir offices [**2.11 lines 12–13**]
4 (a) What do **2.11** and **2.13** reveal about Jesuit attitudes towards social problems?
  (b) Explain why **2.13** was 'holy work' [**line 13**].
5 'We are the militia of Christ' (St Ignatius, 1539):
  (a) What in Ignatius' background helps explain his attitude to Jesuit organisation?
  (b) According to **2.10**, what did Ignatius originally intend his followers to do?
  (c) Do you find it surprising that the combating of Protestantism barely figures in **2.11**? Explain your answer.
  (d) How does **2.12** enable us to understand the purpose of the 'militia'?

Problems in the reform of existing orders: reformer versus reformer

Reform among existing orders was rarely plain sailing. Vested interests blocked, delayed or neutralised reform initiatives, but it was not only the unreformed who made waves. Reformers sometimes got in each other's way. From 1539, Paul III was reforming the old orders by papal commission. One of the first he tackled was the Lateran Congregation of the Canons Regular of St Augustine, a group of 60 Italian houses. Their Protector, Cardinal Gonzaga, was something of a reformer himself, but Paul appointed the zealous Cardinal Contarini to mastermind operations. The result was an overlap of jurisdiction. Gonzaga took offence and the project was nearly stillborn.

Matteo da Bascio discovered a different problem. He was a Franciscan who, in 1525, left his friary to live a stricter religious life. Three years later he won papal approval to turn his fledgling community into a separate Franciscan order, the Capuchins, and by 1535 he had attracted 700 recruits, many of them fellow Franciscans. The trouble was that the friars he had left and rejected, accusing them of betraying the primitive simplicity and poverty of their founder, were themselves 'observants' (reformed). His concept of reform challenged the integrity of others and could only be interpreted as an act of disobedience threatening rebellion and schism within the order. When one person's ardour was another's complacency, there was bound to be trouble.

2.14   Reform: how to bypass obstruction

His Holiness has resolved to appoint me Vice-Protector ... We need sound
information. It is no good attempting to interfere in their Chapter General
without further investigation: we tried that here in Rome in the election of the
General of the Friars Minor ... I have decided to write secretly to two trusty
Lateran canons, commanding them on their vow of obedience that they tell me   5
the truth about the disorders in the Congregation, both in general and in
particular; advise me what remedies seem good to them; give me the names of
those canons who are able, upright and experienced from whom we may obtain
sound information; and observe the strictest silence about the whole affair ...
Meanwhile, let them hold their Chapter. When we are soundly informed we shall   10
proceed by extraordinary commission and overwhelm them.

Cardinal Contarini to Cardinal Gonzaga, March 1540, in P. McNair, *Peter*
Martyr in Italy: An Anatomy of Apostasy, **Clarendon Press, by permission**
of Oxford University Press, 1967, pp. 186–7

2.15   Reformers in conflict

Your solution regarding the Canons looks as though it were proposed on purpose
to insult me ... I appealed to you in the first place for help because you are near
the Pope and able to point out to his Beatitude the troubles which are found in
the Congregation. But you have failed me. I find myself much deceived. Rather
than helping me, you preferred to tackle the reform yourself, taking it upon you 5
to consult everyone, even the Bishop of Verona, except me. I just do not know
what has got into your head. I have been Protector for twelve years and by my
authority can extract more truth from these Canons by one word than anyone
else in a thousand. They fear me.

Cardinal Gonzaga to Cardinal Contarini, May 1540, in McNair, *Peter*
Martyr, **pp. 188–9**

2.16   In defence of Capuchin strictness

If it is objected that to separate the good from the bad is to ruin the Order, I
certainly do not intend that. But the unity of the Order demands uniformity of
observance; in them must be one heart and one soul. It is not so with the
Observants. Hence it is necessary that His Holiness should make regulations for
the few good brethren that they may be free to walk in the stricter path, as did   5
Eugenius IV[1] and has been recently done in Spain and Portugal; and that places
be assigned to these brethren which shall be to them cities of refuge where they
can observe the Rule. But such relief must come from the Holy See, not from

the General or the General Chapter, for it is known that friars wishing to observe
the Rule strictly have been dispersed amongst the unreformed and treated as   10
fools.

¹ Pope Eugenius (1431–47) approved the separation of reformed ('observants') and
unreformed ('conventuals').

**Giampetro Carafa, Superior of the Theatines (later Pope Paul IV),
August 1532, quoted in Father Cuthbert, *The Capuchins: A Contribution
to the History of the Counter-Reformation*, Sheed and Ward, London, 1928,
I, p. 77**

2.17   Strictness rejected: the Capuchins disbanded

The friars calling themselves Capuchins withdraw from the houses of the
Observance and dwell in various places where they live a life so exceedingly
austere and rigid that it is hardly human, and thus greatly disturb the minds of
other members of the [Franciscan] Order who in consequence doubt whether
they themselves are equally satisfying the obligations of the Rule: thus many are   5
scandalized.

The ban was lifted in 1535 but, until 1574, the order was forbidden to settle outside Italy.

Papal Brief of Clement VII, May 1534, in Cuthbert, *The Capuchins*, I, p. 82

Questions

1   (a) What obstacles did **2.14** anticipate in reforming the canons?
    (b) How did he propose to bypass them?
2   (a) Why did Cardinal Gonzaga **[2.15]** so object to Cardinal Contarini's
         scheme **[2.14]**?
    (b) Does the penultimate sentence in **2.14** undermine Gonzaga's credibility
         as a reformer?
3   From **2.16** and **2.17**, explain why the early Capuchins faced such
    opposition.

Changing attitudes in Rome

In theory, western Christendom was a single spiritual unit, under the pope
as Vicar of Christ and Patriarch of the West. In fact, administration and
management were shared with secular rulers. The 15th century saw a considerable recovery by kings of their ancient participation in regulating the

church and, in direct consequence, the church's ability to control its own affairs was diminished. Even so, the pope still headed an organisation run along strictly hierarchical lines. Without the papacy adopting the reformist cause and directing it, Catholic reform would never progress beyond the piecemeal. Yet the papacy of 1500 had become heavily politicised and those political activities dangerously compromised its spiritual authority. Traditional explanations of papal worldliness and corruption, indifference and inertia are all valid. From the death of Pius II in 1464, popes were conspicuous for their lack of commitment to reformation. Most assisted individual projects, if asked, but the initiative and drive always came from outside Rome. Several popes established reform commissions, but none delivered, either because their concern represented no more than a passing twinge of conscience (e.g. Alexander VI) or, as with Pius III (1503) and Adrian VI (1522–3), because their reigns were too short. Indeed, most people despaired of papal-led reform – hence the patchwork of individual, localised initiatives that have made up this chapter.

Apocalyptic expectation had, however, placed the papacy in a spotlight. Some prophets suggested that the greatest threat to Christendom came from within and, when Rome failed, the last days were imminent. Then came the Sack of Rome (1527) when Clement VII played one trick too many in the switchback of Italian power politics. Widely interpreted in Rome as divine punishment for the sins of the papacy, the Sack shattered the indifference of many in high places. The new tone was evident from the moment Paul III was elected in October 1534. Himself an old-style political, pleasure-loving pope, he nonetheless sensed the need for corporate action, for comprehensive papal-led renewal. Fortunately his reign, to 1549, was the longest of the century. Among the many reformers he promoted to the college of cardinals was Gasparo Contarini, a move which 'gave to the reform movement a solid centre' (Jedin, 1957). Nonetheless, the reformers still represented only a minority view and hope was tempered with realism: 'In the pope we have an extraordinary leader. Alas he is no stronger than the depravity of the times' (Cardinal Sadoleto, 1538).

Pressed hard by Charles V, Paul III in April 1536 convoked a general council to assemble the following year [4.4]. By way of preparation, the pope appointed a Commission of Nine. Their deliberations produced the famed *Consilium de emendanda ecclesia*, a 'warts and all' report on the state of the church and the means of regeneration. That the *Consilium* confined its eyes to Italy reveals how myopic still was the view from the papal heights. Germany and Protestants did not figure in their thinking. That in itself, however, serves to remind us once again that the agenda of reform was not set and dictated by the Reformation. And what was true of the diocese of Rome was true of every other. 'The air of Rome was pregnant with reform' as Contarini and his circle 'guided the destinies of the Roman church' (McNair, 1967 and 1981).

2.18   A papal confession

God has allowed this punishment[1] to overtake His church because of the sins of men, especially those of priests and prelates ... There have been great spiritual abominations and abuses in the Holy See for many years. Perversion has grown everywhere and it is hardly surprising that the sickness has spread from the head to the members. Every single one of us has fallen victim. Not even one of us has   5
done good ... We will do everything in our power to reform first this See, from which the powerful evil advanced so that, even as corruption passed from Rome to every other part, so healing will spread from Rome. The whole world eagerly desires reform and we are definitely responsible ... Be patient. Every error and abuse will not be swept away at once; the disease is well established. Therefore   10
progress must be made step by step ... lest everything become still more chaotic.

[1] 'this punishment' = the fall of Belgrade and Rhodes to the Turks.

Adrian VI to the Diet of Nuremberg, January 1523, in *Documents Illustrative of the Continental Reformation*, **ed. B. J. Kidd, Clarendon Press, Oxford, 1911, p. 109†**

2.19   Divine punishment: the Sack of Rome

You must understand just how wicked are these days and how angry is Heaven at the rabble now admitted everywhere to the exalted office of the priesthood (lazy, untrained, disorganised and immoral, mere youths, bankers, merchants and soldiers, not to mention usurers and pimps) ... The Emperor's army, tearing to pieces the barbaric filth, have overthrown and burnt everything in this dunghill.   5
They have triumphed over pride, wealth and power. The ungodly say 'If God cares for sacred things, why does he allow this?' I reply that it is because God cares that he not only allows this thing, but even carries it out himself.

Cardinal Giles of Viterbo, *Scechina e Libellus,* **c. 1529, in J. W. O'Malley,** *Giles of Viterbo on Church and Reform: A Study in Renaissance Thought,* **E. J. Brill, Leiden, 1968, p. 133**

2.20   The verdict of the papal commission

The spirit of God decrees that Christ's church, almost collapsed, should be restored to its early glory ... Your Holiness knows that these evils arose from the

wilfulness of several previous popes ... [and their belief] that the pope, being lord
of all benefices, can sell his own and cannot therefore be guilty of simony ...
From this, as the Trojan horse, burst forth into God's Church so many grave ills   5
... [which] obeying your command we have examined and here make known to
you ...

Concerning ordination: no care is taken. Whoever they are (uneducated, of
appalling morals, under age), they are routinely admitted to the holy order from
which came so many scandals and a contempt for the church. Reverence for   10
divine service is so much diminished as now to be virtually extinct ... Your
Holiness should order every bishop to take the greatest care in this and,
observing the laws, appoint a professor to instruct their clergy in letters and in
morals ... [11 paragraphs detailing abuses relating to benefices.]

Another common abuse is the conferring of bishoprics on the most reverend   15
cardinals. These offices are incompatible. Cardinals should assist Your Holiness
in Rome whereas bishops must care for their flocks and so be resident with them
as the shepherd. This sets a particularly harmful example for how can the Holy
See correct the abuses of others if abuse is tolerated in its own senior ranks? And
as they are cardinals they have not greater freedom to break the law but far less.   20
Their life should be as a law to all others ... yet what can they encourage in
others but greed? ... Heavy penalties should be imposed, especially withholding of
income ...

Concerning the government of the Christian faithful, the most fundamental
abuse in need of reformation is that bishops and priests must not be absent from   25
their churches, but must be resident for they are entrusted with their care. What
sight can be more piteous than deserted churches? Almost all the shepherds have
deserted their flocks or abandoned them to hirelings. A heavy penalty must be
imposed, not only censures but the withholding of income ... [on all] absent for
more than three Sundays per year ...   30

An intolerable abuse lies in the impediments put in the way of bishops ruling
their flocks. Many evil-doers are exempt from their jurisdiction ... Among these,
none are more blatant than the monastic orders, who are become so deformed
that they do grave harm by example. All conventuals should be done away with,
by the prohibition of admitting novices ... [10 paragraphs detailing the evils of   35
dispensations and indulgences.]

Concerning Rome: honest manners should flourish in this city and church,
mother and teacher of other churches ... [yet] whores perambulate like matrons,
or ride on mule-back, with whom noblemen, cardinals and priests consort in
broad daylight.

The principal authors of this report were Cardinals Contarini and Carafa.

Consilium de emendanda ecclesia, **March 1537, in Kidd,** *Documents*, **pp.
307–18†**

Questions

1 (a) From **2.1** and **2.18**, explain reformist interest in the Ottomans.
   (b) How convincing do you find Adrian VI's confession in **2.18**?
   (c) Assess the advantages and disadvantages for reform of this approach.
2 Do you find the attitude in **2.19** surprising? Explain your answer.
3 Answer the following with reference to **2.20**:
   (i)   What was the top priority? Would Adrian VI [**2.18**] have agreed?
   (ii)   Does a sense of urgency underpin the *Consilium*?
   (iii) Why do you suppose that it did not deal with doctrinal questions?
   (iv) 'The *Consilium* recommended monasticism be abolished' (Trevor-Roper, 1966). Is that true?
   (v)   What do **lines 9–15** suggest was the effectiveness of **2.8(c)**?
   (vi)   Was episcopal non-residence more the fault of kings than popes?
   (vii) Why should the state of the city of Rome be relevant?
   (viii) Was it a weakness that its authors all lived in Rome?
4 'The *Consilium* will not reform the church, but destroy it. This is not reform but revolution' (Bartolomeo Guidiccioni, papal vicar of Parma and adviser to Paul III, 1538). How does this help us to understand:
   (i)   the aims of **2.20**
   (ii) papal failure to implement it?
5 From your wider reading, assess Paul III's contribution to Catholic renewal.

Summary

1 Is your assessment of the state of the church (from Chapter 2) compatible with your verdict (from Chapter 1) on the state of religion? Explain your answer.
2 When studying the late medieval church, how helpful are the following observations:
   (i)   'The similar content of so much reformist complaint reflects as much the thoughtless repetition of propagandist stereotypes as the stubborn persistence of the alleged abuses' (Oakley, *The Western Church in the Later Middle Ages*, 1979)
   (ii) 'Reformers attacked clerical failings to protect the integrity of ecclesiastical authority' (O'Malley, *Giles of Viterbo on Church and Reform*, 1968)

(iii) 'The ability of the church to regulate its own affairs now depended primarily on the secular state rather than popes, councils and bishops' (Dickens, *The Counter Reformation*, 1968)

Justify your answers with reference to the texts in this chapter.

References

H. Baron, 'Religion and Politics in the German Imperial Cities', *English Historical Review*, LII, 1937

F. Cesareo, *Humanism and Catholic Reform: the Life and Work of Gregorio Cortese*, Peter Lang, New York, 1990

P. Chaunu, *The Reformation*, Alan Sutton, 1989

A. Dickens, *The Counter Reformation*, Thames and Hudson, 1968

I. Green, 'Reformed Pastors and *Bons Curés*: The Changing Role of the Parish Clergy in Early Modern Europe', *Studies in Church History*, XXVI, 1989

J. Haller, *Papsttum und Kirchenreform*, Berlin, 1903

P. McNair, *Peter Martyr in Italy: An Anatomy of Apostasy*, Clarendon Press, 1967

P. McNair, 'The Reformation of the Sixteenth Century in Renaissance Italy', *Studies in Church History*, XVII, 1981

J. O'Malley, *Giles of Viterbo on Church and Reform*, E. J. Brill, Leiden, 1968

A. Renaudet, *Humanisme et renaissance*, Droz, Geneva, 1958

E. Rice, *The Foundations of Early Modern Europe, 1460–1559*, Weidenfeld, 1970

T. Tentler, *Sin and Confession on the Eve of the Reformation*, Princeton University Press, 1977

H. R. Trevor-Roper, *Historical Essays*, Harper & Row, 1966

For Evennett (1968), Jedin, Oakley, O'Malley (1993) and Scarisbrick, see *Suggestions for further reading*.

3 Countering the Reformation 1517–45

The Reformation swept with astonishing speed across Germany and beyond. This chapter examines why, before the Council of Trent, the Catholic church was not more successful in halting or slowing down the Protestant onslaught. Most who supported Luther in the early years misunderstood him, responding to the polemical or negative aspects of his message. They saw a reformer of church abuses, a champion of new learning, a patriot defending Germany. These pseudo-protestantisms were, until the mid-1520s, a real problem for Rome because they turned the heresy into a mass movement. But the situation did not improve as the misunderstandings cleared. Chapter 1 showed the late medieval hunger for assurance of salvation. Luther had found a non-medieval solution that assuaged those medieval anxieties and made redundant the church's sacramental system: justification by faith. In that therapeutic power of Protestant theology to liberate people from fear lay the greater threat.

Against Martin Luther, 1517–21

Luther died in bed in 1546, not at the stake in 1518. Historians agree that proceedings against him could have been swifter, more powerful, more effective. The consequences are of the greatest significance. There might still have been a Reformation, but without Luther it must have been very different. Two points should be borne in mind when judging the initial Catholic response. First, Luther set the agenda: as his thought developed, so counter-measures were necessarily reactive. Second, the transformation of a provincial academic debate into the most damaging rupture in Christendom for centuries surprised both sides. Indulgences were controversial because medieval salvation theology was vague and Luther was not the first to raise legitimate doubts. His attack had, however, enraged the powerful Dominican Order, those great sponsors of indulgences, hunters of heresy and promoters of papal authority. In December 1517 he was reported to Rome. Papal investigations began in May 1518 and, two months later, Luther was summoned to appear for trial in Rome within 60 days, not for questioning indulgences but for diminishing the power of the pope.

3.1 Authority endangered

3.1(a)

The Roman Church can decide on questions of faith and custom. Those decisions have the force of law. When the pontiff makes a decision as pope, he speaks the infallible rule of faith. He who rejects that doctrine of the Roman Church, from which Holy Scripture draws strength and authority, is a heretic ... He who thinks incorrectly concerning the teachings and practices of the Church,   5
or who says that the Church may not grant indulgences as it does now,[1] is a heretic.

[1] The papal constitution *Cum postquam* (1518) rejected Luther's criticisms of indulgences.

Prierias was papal theologian and drafted the prosecution case against Luther.

Sylvester Prierias, a Dominican, *Dialogue against the Arrogant Theses of Martin Luther*, Rome, 1518, in *Martini Lutheri Opera Latini*, Frankfurt, 1865, I, pp. 346–7†

3.1(b)

Luther's erroneous article will encourage many people to despise the might and authority of his Papal Holiness and of the Holy Roman See. They will neglect the work of sacramental satisfaction. They will never now believe the preachers and doctors. Everyone will interpret Scripture as takes his fancy. And all sacred Christendom must come into great spiritual danger when each individual believes   5
what pleases him most.

Johann Tetzel, a Dominican, *Vorlegung gemacht wyder eynen vormessen sermon*, April 1518

3.1(c)

Where are almost all the Asian churches? Gone. Why? (Let Germany hear this; let the world understand why these churches are no more.) Because they separated themselves from their head, and strayed from their shepherd, and were encouraged to seek equality with their mother the Roman church ... Where are all the churches of the Greeks and Armenians? They have perished. Why? For the   5
same reason ... Germany, Saxony! Who has so bewitched you that you do not see this?

Ambrosius Catharinus, a Dominican, *An Apology for the Truth of the Catholic and Apostolic Faith against the Impious and Pestilential teachings of*

Martin Luther, Florence, 1518, both in D. V. N. Bagchi, *Luther's Earliest Opponents: Catholic Controversialists 1518–1528*, Augsburg Fortress Press, Minneapolis, 1991, pp. 33–4, 63

3.2 Seize Luther!

To prevent this pest from infecting the minds of the simple ... compel Martin to appear personally before you. Call on the assistance of our beloved son Maximilian, the other German princes and cities. When you have Martin, keep him under safe guard ... If he comes of his own accord, showing signs of hearty repentance, we give you power of kindly receiving him into our holy mother church ... [If] he comes not, declare in public edict that he and his followers are heretics, excommunicated and accursed. You may by our authority, and under pain of excommunication, require all prelates, princes, counts, barons, cities and magistrates that, as they desire to be considered Christians, they should seize all his adherents and give them into your charge ... [If they] receive Martin or his adherents in any way, or should give the said Martin aid, counsel or favour, openly or secretly, directly or indirectly, we subject their cities, towns and domains to the interdict as well.

5

10

Leo X to Cardinal Cajetan, papal nuncio in Germany, 23 August 1518, in *Luther's Correspondence and other Contemporary Letters*, ed. P. Smith, Philadelphia, 1913, I, pp. 102–4

Luther's fate depended on his prince, the elector of Saxony. Devout Catholic though he was, Frederick the Wise was 'a proud prince on the colonial frontier of Europe, more jealous than most for his sovereignty' (Barraclough, 1946). He had already banned papal indulgences, denounced papal taxes and was not about to admit a papal warrant. Against such a spirit, Rome's best efforts would founder: 'The supreme ecclesiastical authority of the German prince was not a result of the Reformation; it preceded it' (Oberman, 1989). Rome wooed Frederick, but the death of Maximilian I further weakened the papal hand. As one of the seven electors, the Saxon prince's vote in the coming imperial election was crucial to the political interests of Leo X. So Rome made concessions, agreeing that Luther could be judged in Germany, by German bishops.

3.3 Papal lobbying

It has come to our ears that a certain son of iniquity, Friar Martin, forgetting his profession which consists in humility and obedience, sinfully vaunts himself in the Church and, as though relying on your protection, fears the authority of no one. Although we know this is false, yet we thought good to write to your

lordship ... exhorting you, in the Lord, that for the name and fame of a Catholic   5
prince such as you are, you should retain the splendour of your glory and race
unsullied by these calumnies ... As this affair concerns the purity of the faith of
God and the Catholic church, and it is the proper office of the Apostolic See to
take cogniscence of who thinks rightly and who wrongly, we exhort your
lordship, for the sake of God's honour and ours and your own, please to give   10
help that this Martin be delivered into the power and judgement of the Holy See.

**Leo X to Frederick the Wise, 23 August 1518, in Smith, *Luther's
Correspondence*, I, p. 105**

3.4   Conspiracy exposed

There is an extraordinary conspiracy of those who hate liberal studies, which can
have no result except to harm good, pious, educated men. That the Lutheran
cause should not be condemned by the learned and that Dr Martin's works
should be eagerly read by all men of good will in your part of the world[1] is a joy
to us; all the more because most men of good will and learning in our countries   5
and principalities, to say nothing of foreign parts, write in praise of his life and
character no less than his scholarship ... The last thing we wish is to lay penalties
upon those who deserve rewards. Nor, with the help of Almighty God, shall we
ever so act that through our fault any innocent man is handed to the impious
keeping of those who seek only their own advantage.

[1] 'your part of the world' – Erasmus was in the Netherlands.

**Frederick the Wise to Erasmus, May 1519, in Mynors and Thomson,
Erasmus, VI, p. 355**

Proceedings were resumed in February 1520. The bull *Exsurge domine*
condemning Luther's teachings was published in June; his excommunication
followed in January 1521. Meanwhile, as Rome manoeuvred, heresy prospered. Rather than wonder what more could have been done, consider
whether Rome's greater mistake was to have picked the wrong target? Luther
was by temperament deferential and conservative. He was no innovator,
certainly no revolutionary. Instead of attacking the abusers of indulgences,
they tried to destroy the reformer. By treating Luther so aggressively, so
negatively, had Rome manufactured the breach?

3.5   Luther's excommunication

Many who followed Martin took cognizance of our missive [*Exsurge domine*] and
its warnings, confessed their errors and abjured the heresy ... In several states,
books of the said Martin were publicly burned, as we had enjoined ... Our

decrees are passed against Martin and others who follow him, against those who
protect him with a military bodyguard, and presume to afford help, counsel and   5
favour toward him. All their names and rank, however lofty and dazzling their
dignity, we wish to be taken as included with the same effect as if they were
individually listed. On all these we decree the sentence of excommunication, of
anathema, of our perpetual condemnation and interdict; of privation of dignities,
honours and property on them and their descendants ... We enjoin every   10
archbishop and prelate make themselves as a wall of defence for their Christian
people. They shall not keep silence like dumb dogs that cannot bark, but
incessantly cry and lift up their voice, preaching and causing to be preached the
word of God and the truth of the Catholic faith.

Decet Romanum, **papal bull of Leo X, in Rupp and Drewery,** *Martin
Luther*, **pp. 63–6**

Questions

1 (a) Explain the meaning of 'the work of sacramental satisfaction'
        [**3.1(b) line 3**]
   (b) On what grounds do **3.1(a)–(c)** attack Luther?
2 (a) Why might Rome not have considered Frederick a good son of the
        church?
   (b) Explain why **3.2** and **3.3** are so different in tone.
   (c) From **3.4** and your wider reading, explain why Frederick defied
        Rome.
3 (a) Should we be sceptical of the first sentence in **3.5**?
   (b) Consider how far **3.5** is an admission of papal failure.
4 'In the heat of controversy, both sides were forced into positions, at
   times extreme and unbalanced, from which retreat with honour was
   impossible' (Ozment, *The Reformation in the Cities*, 1975). How far do
   3.1–3.5 show this was true of Catholicism?

Anti-Reformation: censorship and propaganda

If Catholic power could not silence the messenger, it became imperative to
silence the message. Control of printing became crucial to the success of
anti-Reformation. Most printers were, however, sympathetic to the heresy
and, silently, unobtrusively, their output slithered everywhere; by 1521,
there were over 300,000 Lutheran books and pamphlets in circulation from
Hungary to France. Consumer demand alone, it seemed, would determine
the outcome. As yet, there was no central bureau for censorship. Rather it
was the responsibility of bishops, individually. They were simply over-

whelmed and, as loyal Catholic authorities struggled, the personal commitment of secular rulers usually proved decisive. At the same time, Catholics
themselves needed to use the press, but pro-Catholic authors faced an uphill
struggle. They lacked co-ordination and leadership; their only significant
financial supporter was Duke George of Albertine Saxony. Even allowing for
poor sales, they printed, and preached, far too little. Targeted very narrow-
ly at the clergy, princes and councillors, their works were too scholarly, too
defensive, and far too rarely tried to show why Protestantism was wrong.

How are we to explain Catholicism's conspicuous failure in the early
propaganda war? The church hierarchy saw the heresy as primarily a law and
order problem, to be tackled not by commissioning books, but by empower-
ing inquisitors. Unlike the heretics, the Catholics had everything to lose
by a war of words. To debate with Protestants would be to admit there were
issues to discuss; any such dialogue would only grant credibility and legit-
imacy to their claims. Indeed, not a few bishops and princes believed
Decet Romanum had banned works of controversy. Rome had spoken.
Protestantism had been condemned. Nothing further was required.

3.6 Censorship in the Empire

None shall have, sell, give, read, leave in churches or other places any writings
(published or to be published) by Luther, Wyclif, Hus, Oecolampadius, Zwingli,
Melanchthon or others of their sect, the New Testament, Gospels, Epistles or
Prophets in French or German with prefaces or notes or doctrines condemned by
or contrary to our holy faith. None shall make, draw or have scandalous models,   5
images or pictures of the Blessed Virgin Mary or the saints ... Equally, none shall
print books on scripture, the faith or the church without first having obtained a
licence from the local magistrate. Any who violate these decrees are a peril to the
realm and shall be executed, men by the sword, women by being buried alive.

**Charles V, edict of 1540, in *Apologie de Guillaume de Nassau, Prince
d'Orange*, ed. A. Lacroix, Brussels, 1858, pp. 268–72†**

3.7 No censorship in Sweden

3.7(a)

By the allegiance which I owe you, I deem it my duty to urge you not to allow
the sale of Luther's books within the realm, nor give his pupils shelter or
encouragement of any kind, till the coming church council shall pass its
judgement ... I know not how your Grace can better win the love of God, as well
as of all Christian princes.

3.7(b)

Regarding your request that we forbid the sale of Luther's writings, we know not
by what right it could be done, for we are told his teachings have not yet been
found by impartial judges to be false. Moreover, since writings opposed to Luther
have been circulated throughout the land, it seems but right that his too should
be kept public, that you and other scholars may detect their fallacies and show   5
them to the people. Then the books of Luther may be condemned.

3.7(a) Bishop Hans Brask of Linkoping to King Gustav Vasa, May 1524
3.7(b) The King's reply, June 1524, both in Kidd, *Documents*, p. 153

3.8   Protestant perversion of the Bible

This disgraceful fellow [Luther] has deliberately perverted, omitted from and
added to the ancient authentic text of the church. He has forced different
meanings and added many annoying glosses ... Emser[1] accordingly published a
special pamphlet in which he not only collected all the erroneous glosses,
perversions and falsifications in Luther's translation, but also made available at   5
the same time as acceptable medicine against Luther's poison a version which
agrees with the accepted and established Latin text of the church. This was to
the special comfort of the Catholics who, with the help of this pamphlet, could
see and understand Luther's dangerous errors and counter the evangelical
glorying and boasting of the Lutheran fools. But before Emser's work saw the   10
light of day, Luther's Testament had been so propagated by the printers that
even tailors and shoemakers, indeed women and other simple idiots, though they
could read only a little German, read it eagerly as if it were a fountain of all truth
... [and] without timidity they debated not only with Catholic laymen, but also
with priests and monks ... These Lutheran women, lacking all female modesty,   15
arrogantly usurped the office of preaching.

[1] Jerome Emser's illustrated German New Testament (1525) masqueraded as a Protestant
edition, but was full of anti-Protestant notes.

Johann Cochläus, secretary and chaplain to Duke George of Saxony,
Commentaries on the Acts and Writings of Martin Luther*, 1549, in *The
***Reformation in its own Words*, ed. H. J. Hillerbrand, SCM Press Ltd,**
London, 1964, pp. 386–7

3.9   Protestant perversion of the social fabric

As Luther has denied to the successor of St Peter the right to guide the flock so
he will eventually withdraw from every prince the right to exercise judgement,
pass sentences, enforce settlements or promulgate laws, and will contend that all
things pertain to all people. And he will come to reject punishment, and will free

everyone from the rule of law, and the evil and wicked from fear of the same,   5
and will give them the very worst kind of liberty.

**Thomas Rhadinus, a Dominican, *To the Illustrious Princes of Germany*,
Leipzig, 1520, in Bagchi, *Luther's Earliest Opponents*, p. 100**

3.10   Missing the target

Unlike all the rest, you[1] alone have attacked the real issues and have not wearied
me with irrelevancies about the papacy, purgatory, indulgences and such trifles –
for trifles they are rather than the main issue ... The human will is like a beast of
burden. If God rides it, it wills as God wills; if Satan rides it it wills and goes as
Satan wills. Nor can it choose its rider. It is the riders who contend for the   5
possession ... Free choice without the grace of God is not free at all, but
immutably the captive and slave of evil, since it cannot itself turn to good ... If
we believe that Christ has redeemed men by his blood, we are bound to confess
that the whole man was lost.

[1] 'you' = Erasmus; Luther here was answering his *Diatribe on Free Will*, which argued for
free will and human co-operation with God in salvation.

**Luther, *On the Enslaved Will*, 1525, in *Luther's Works*, ed. J. Pelikan and
H. Lehmann, Augsburg Fortress Press, Minneapolis, 1957, XXXIII, pp.
294, 293**

Questions

1 (a) Identify the authors banned in **3.6**.
   (b) Did **3.6** ban vernacular bibles? Explain your answer.
   (c) Since Protestants did not produce images mocking the Virgin,
        consider what **lines 5–6** in **3.6** could have in mind (read **6.6**
        before you answer).
2 Contrast the attitudes to Protestantism in **3.6** and **3.7(b)**.
3 (a) 'As if ... of all truth' [**3.8 line 13**]. Why should that be said?
   (b) Explain the meaning of 'glosses' [**3.8 line 3**].
   (c) Is **3.8** an argument against **2.2–2.3**? Justify your response.
4 Consider what **3.6**, **3.8** and **3.9** reveal about Catholic perceptions of
   Protestantism.
5 What do **3.8–3.9** tell us about the audience targeted by pro-Catholics?
6 (a) What, according to **3.10** were 'the real issues' [**line 1**]?
   (b) How far do **3.1–3.9** indicate that Catholic and Protestant were
        following different agendas? Explain your answer.

A question of leadership

The church hierarchy

When in *Decet Romanum* Leo X appealed for 'a wall of defence', he looked to the bishops. The administrative structure of the church meant that bishops, effectively area managers, were ideally placed to stamp out heresy as soon as it emerged. Yet episcopal zeal was, too often, inadequate and episcopal behaviour could 'border on sabotage' (Jedin, 1957). Powerful currents sapped anti-Reformation north of the Alps, but as many in Italy despaired of Germany's clergy so papal enterprise was judged woefully inadequate on both sides of the mountains. In a church where authority was so hierarchically structured, Rome's failings were the more lethal.

In Rome, everything began to change with the election of Paul III in October 1534. How far he understood the religious situation outside Italy is uncertain, but he recognised Catholicism's nakedness. That marked a watershed. The catalyst was probably the emergence of Protestantism in Italy and it gave rise to what must be the most extraordinary example of anti-Reformation. Paul appointed Cardinal Contarini to direct a counter-offensive across six dioceses. As we have seen, Contarini was a Catholic evangelical and the campaign he organised aimed to beat the Protestants at their own game, using justification by faith and other biblically based teaching for the benefit of Rome. In tactics (though not theology), this was no different to the famed Jesuit missions launched later that century. Contarini's was not in place long enough, however, for us to make comparison. The evangelical aim to graft Lutheran insights on to a reformed Catholicism proved difficult to balance and everything crashed when Contarini's star preachers [3.13 lines 1–2] became Protestants, fleeing Italy in August 1542. Their defections made the balance impossible to hold.

3.11   Awkward bishops?

Was there any examination of the matter here? The peace of Germany is disturbed with 'heresy, heresy' when, in truth, the Wittenberg affair is no more than a schoolroom quarrel. They run with the smell of blood in their noses and would make another Reuchlin[1] ... When have we heard or read such notions? Those Dominican flatterers would so exalt His Holiness as to make bishops no   5 more than hireling vicars ... That there must be a council all here are agreed. The council is the place to hear Luther and settle this matter.

[1] Johann Reuchlin (d. 1522) was a scholar pursued by the Dominicans as a heretic for encouraging the study of Hebrew.

Gabriel von Eyb, Bishop of Eichstadt to the Bishop of Verona, May 1522, in *Zeitschrift für Kirchengeschichte*, XIX, 1899, pp. 478–9†

3.12   Apathetic popes?

Obviously you think that our cause needs no further aid – no bulls, letters or speeches to bishops or to princes. Clearly you believe that force and threat are unnecessary in Germany. How then do you intend to bring victory to the Catholic cause? What secret plan are you preparing? A conspiracy perhaps, or poison slipped into Luther's beer? Some clever trick – yes, some clever trick; that   5 must be it ... Rome has been so silent, so inactive that the heretics must believe a great scheme is being planned. Oh that they were right!

Johann Cochläus to the papal nuncio in Germany, September 1526, in *Zeitschrift für Kirchengeschichte*, XVIII, 1898, p. 120†

3.13   To combat Protestantism: an unorthodox formula

By gentleness and eloquence, the preachers will hold your people, as Vermigli[1] in Lucca and the General[2] in Modena. We are charged to keep these souls within the one church where alone salvation may be found. So if we are to bring peace and assurance to endangered souls, we must preach the foundations of religion. By faith in Christ crucified we are saved and through his merits alone we are   5 redeemed ... Reparation for sin must be paid, both now through the most sweet sacrament[3] and later in the holy fire of purgatory ... At the same time, the diseases which have brought low Christ's Church must be rooted out. Apply your hand to the ruins around you.

[1] Pietro Vermigli (d. 1562), Augustinian Prior of S. Frediano, Lucca.
[2] Bernardino Ochino (d. 1564), Vicar-General of the Capuchins.
[3] 'the most sweet sacrament' = penance.

Cardinal Contarini to Cardinal Gonzaga, Bishop of Mantua, March 1542, in F. Dittrich, *Regesten und Briefe des Kardinals Contarini*, Braunsberg, 1881, pp. 360–1†

Secular rulers

Monarchs and city councils could, just like peasants, feel bewildered, outraged and threatened by Protestantism. To the success or failure of anti-

Reformation, the attitude of secular rulers was invariably critical for ecclesiastical authority was never enough to hold the front single-handedly. The firm rule of Wittelsbach dukes in Bavaria and Habsburg archdukes in Austria served as a thin Catholic line which, almost alone, kept central Europe for Rome. Where there was no great prince in Germany and Switzerland, elected councils determined for or against the Reformation. Cities like Bamberg and Paderborn could act to clip the powers of their local clergy and improve urban preaching – issues high on the agenda of every council – without using Protestantism to do it. In several, like Würzburg and Cologne, 'the vital ingredient of a broadly based popular movement was forestalled by the Peasants War' (Cameron, 1991). Fear of disorder led these councils, invariably encouraged by the local bishop or abbot, to keep a tight rein on guilds and other fermentors of agitation. In the Swiss city of Zug, on the other hand, it was the citizens themselves who decided the issue, voting to remain Catholic. Motives varied enormously, as they did among those endorsing the new creed. However, we should not underestimate the importance of tradition and innate conservatism when analysing Catholic loyalties. What was essential was for the authorities to act quickly and decisively to defend the old religion and silence the preachers. Only that could forestall an alliance forming between reform ideas and guild grievances; if such a union was formed, Protestant advance was virtually inevitable.

3.14   A rite of purification

During the night [1 June 1528], heretics cut the head from a statue of the Virgin and Child at a street corner ... When the king heard of this, he was so shocked that he wept. He made a proclamation that anyone with information must inform the authorities and offered a reward of one thousand gold crowns ... On 12 [June], processions came from every parish ... carrying banners, crosses and sacred relics   5
to St Catherine's for mass. The king was bareheaded and held a large white candle, as did all the noblemen. The Bishop of Lisieux carried a beautiful silver statue, two feet tall and commissioned by his majesty. When they reached the site, the king with great humility placed it where the original had been.

Journal d'un bourgeois de Paris sous le règne de François Ier, ed. V. Bourrilly, Paris, 1910, pp. 290–3†

3.15   Dynastic honour

My ancestors were ... until death, faithful sons of the Roman Church. Always they defended the Catholic faith, the sacred ceremonies, decretals, ordinances and holy rites to the honour of God, the propagation of the faith and the salvation of souls. After their deaths they left, by natural law and heritage, these holy Catholic rites, for us to live and to die following their example. I am therefore   5

resolved to maintain everything which these my forebears have established to the
present ... It is certain that a single monk errs in his opinion which is against
what all of Christendom has held for over a thousand years to the present.
According to his opinion all of Christendom has always been in error. To settle
this matter I am therefore determined to use all my dominions and possessions,   10
my friends, my body, my blood, my life and my soul. It would be a great
disgrace for you and me, the illustrious and renowned German nation, appointed
by privilege and singular pre-eminence to be the defenders and protectors of the
Catholic faith, as well as a perpetual dishonour for both us and our posterity, if
in our time not only heresy, but the suspicion of heresy and the degradation of   15
the Christian religion were due to our negligence.

**Charles V addressing the Diet of Worms, April 1521, in Hillerbrand, *The
Reformation*, p. 94**

3.16 Reasons for war

Daily we[1] see this new doctrine advancing ... Nothing good can come from such
perversion, for it results in the destruction of our most holy mother church,
contempt for her services, abuse of God and the Blessed Virgin, mocking of our
protectors the beloved saints, forgetfulness of the souls of the faithful departed
our forefathers ... We will stand against Zurich. We will stand by the ancient   5
faith and root out this Lutheran, Zwinglian false teaching from all our territories.
We stand for God and for liberty. Zurich shall not dictate to us like some new
emperor.

[1] 'we' = the Inner States (Fribourg, Lucerne, Schwyz, Unterwalden and Zug).

**The Beckenried Alliance, April 1524, in *Ämtliche Sammlung der ältern
eidgenossischen Abschiede*, ed. A. von Segesser, Lucerne, 1873, IV (1a), pp.
410–11**

Questions

1 (a) What do you make of the phrase 'Those Dominican ... hireling vicars'
       [3.11 lines 5–6]?
   (b) How do you account for the ideas expressed in **3.11**?
2 Explain how the evidence in this chapter confirms or refutes **3.12**.
3 (a) What does **3.13** refer to by 'the diseases' **[line 8]** and 'the ruins'
       [line 9]?
   (b) Assess **3.13** as a strategy for countering the Reformation.
4 (a) From **3.14** to **3.16**, what can we deduce about motives for remain-
       ing Catholic?
   (b) How far do they tie in with your judgement of **3.8–3.9**?

Conciliation, not confrontation

At what point did the Reformation breach become permanent? As late as 1561, influential figures on both sides believed reunion to be possible. This final section examines the Catholic quest for a negotiated resolution of the Protestant problem. As we have seen, some senior Catholic churchmen believed that Rome had misunderstood Luther. Cardinal Cajetan, the great Dominican theologian, had judged him to be guilty of error, but not of heresy. Could the Catholic church even assess and reject Luther's theology, given its own lack of a defined salvation theology? *Decet Romanum* never tried, and that left room for dialogue. Catholics who took this view did so convinced that, once the rhetoric had been cut away, little of substance divided the two churches. Two different schools of thought held this common position. One was led by Erasmus, then at the height of his influence. He had encouraged Elector Frederick to protect Luther and in the early 1520s he worked 'to extinguish the fires of controversy' (McConica, 1991). Even after his great clash with Luther over free will, Erasmus continued to argue that Catholics and Protestants agreed on all essentials of Christianity, and disagreed only on issues that were *adiaphora* (irrelevant to salvation and therefore indifferent). The second position, itself influenced by Erasmus, was espoused by the *spirituali* or Catholic evangelicals like Cardinal Contarini who considered justification by faith to be the purest Catholicism. For the *spirituali*, the Protestants' sin was not heresy but schism; they had broken the unity of the church and jeopardised her teaching authority. Round-table talks, sponsored by Charles V, provided the main forum for *rapprochement* and the process reached its climax at the Colloquy of Regensburg (1541). Contarini, 'the wisest champion of Catholic liberalism' (McNair, 1967), was appointed by Paul III to head the Catholic delegation. Agreement was speedily reached on several fundamentals of doctrine, notably a theological formula on salvation known as 'double justification'. For a moment, reunion was glimpsed. But other questions proved impossible to resolve and the Colloquy ended in deadlock. Were such talks 'delusive gatherings, hopeless from the beginning' (Jedin, 1957)? Good will was certainly in short supply, on both sides – unlike bigotry. In the short term, it was Contarini's success that mattered, for the Colloquy brought into sharp focus the tension between Catholic reform and anti-Reformation, and symbolised 'the conflict between two different ways of understanding Catholicism itself' (Idigoras, 1969). To men of strife, he seemed disloyal, a dangerous appeaser, perhaps even a crypto-Protestant. His untimely death in August 1542 left the liberals vulnerable and the simultaneous flights of Ochino and Vermigli provided the 'proof' as to their true loyalties. In that moment, 'the mellow balanced sanity of Erasmus' (Phillips, 1981) was routed, and that 'marked the moment of deliverance for the Counter Reformation' (Fenlon, 1972).

3.17 The third party

In search of purity, some trample on holiness, allowing the old church no honour ... In search of security, others defend evil, acknowledging none of the sins that long have afflicted the church ... But there is a third party which, for love of Christ, looks with open eyes and therefore adheres fully to neither side. They desire that Christian truth prevail. Driven by arrogance, each faction sees not that   5
Christ is with the other. Driven by folly, each overlooks Christ and attacks the gospel.

Povel Eliasen, Provincial of the Danish Carmelites, *Against the Malmö Book*, **1530, in C. Secher,** *Povel Eliasens Danske Skrifter*, **Copenhagen, 1855, pp. 345–6†**

3.18 A plea for sanity

The origin of the case is evil: the hatred of letters and the desire for supremacy. The way in which it is being conducted corresponds to the origin, with wild cries, plots, bitter hatred, poisonous writings. Those who are conducting the case are open to suspicion, for the best and closest to the Gospel teaching are said to be the least offended ... The severity of the bull offends all upright men as   5
unworthy of the most gentle Vicar of Christ ... Only two universities[1] out of so countless a number have condemned Luther, and they have merely condemned him, not convicted him of error; nor are they in agreement. Luther is not soliciting anything; there he is less suspect.

[1] Cologne and Louvain, both Dominican controlled.

Erasmus, 'Axiomata', November 1520, in *Christian Humanism and the Reformation*, **ed. J. C. Olin, Harper Collins Publishers Inc, New York, 1965, pp. 147–9**

3.19 Luther is really a Catholic

3.19(a)

Because Luther has said various things on God's grace and about free will, [they] have opposed everything he preaches and teaches about salvation by faith through God's grace and concerning human worthlessness. What they do not see is that, by contradicting Luther, they actually contradict Saints Augustine, Ambrose,

Bernard and Thomas Aquinas. Driven by zeal, their emphatic statements on   5
these matters make them (unwillingly) deviate from Catholic truth.

**Cardinal Contarini to Bishop Giberti of Verona, June 1537, in A. Stella,
'La lettera del Cardinale Contarini sulla predestinazione',** *Rivista di storia
della chiesa in Italia,* **XV, 1961, p. 412†**

3.19(b)

Since therefore the foundation of the Lutheran edifice is true, we must not say
anything against it. We must accept it as true, as Catholic. In fact, we must
accept it as the foundation of Christianity.

**Contarini to Paolo Giustiniani, 1523, in H. Jedin, 'Contarini und
Camaldoli',** *Archivo italiano per la storia della pietà,* **II, 1959, p. 41†**

3.20 'Double justification'

Those who say that we are justified by works speak the truth, and those who say
that we are justified by faith also speak the truth ... Moved by the Holy Spirit,
sinners are justified by a living and effective faith in Our Lord Jesus Christ, not
because of anything within them or because of anything they have done, but only
because God has chosen to give them the justice of Christ ... Only in the merits   5
of Christ can we be confident for in our own actions there are only weakness and
doubt ... Simultaneously, that faith receives the Holy Spirit and is rendered
efficacious in charity, which is an infused gift to heal the will, by which we mean
love for God and for our neighbour. And because justice is also inherent within
man from the creation of Adam, we are called righteous for we do what is   10
rightful. Our renewal is still imperfect and a great weakness still remains. But
God the Father will take that inherent justice and perfect it with the imputed
justice of the Son.

Article 5 of The Regensburg Book, in *Corpus Reformatorum,* **ed. C.
Bretschneider, Halle, 1837, IV, pp. 197–200†**

Questions

1 (a) Why, according to **3.17** and **3.18**, was **3.5** based on false foundations?
   (b) Were Bishops Brask and von Eyb [**3.7(a)**, **3.11**] also Erasmians?
        Explain your answer.
2 How persuasive do you find Contarini's arguments in **3.19**? Justify
   your answer.
3 (a) Summarise the Regensburg formula on justification [**3.20**].
   (b) Does **3.13** teach double justification? Explain your answer.

4   From your wider reading, explain why:
    (i) Regensburg was supported by Charles V, but opposed by Francis I
    (ii) Paul III and Luther agreed to the talks, but probably hoped for
         failure.
5   'For four centuries, Catholic historians denounced Regensburg as
    irresponsible and Protestant scholars dismissed it as delusive' (Hall,
    'The Colloquies between Catholics and Protestants, 1539–41', 1971).
    Why should so many experts have been so anxious to criticise
    Regensburg?

Summary

(i) 'The Protestant claim to be true Catholics and to have restored true
     Catholic Christianity was very dangerous to Rome. It blurred all the
     differences, played on earnest Catholic hopes for reform and encour-
     aged the faithful to see Protestantism and Catholicism as equally valid'
     (Jedin, *History of the Council of Trent*, 1957)
(ii) 'Historically, Regensburg was more significant as a failure than as a
     success. It signified the reality of the Reformation and the necessity of
     the Counter Reformation.' (Fenlon, *Heresy and Obedience in Tridentine
     Italy*, 1972)
Do these statements expose and explain the ultimate failure of anti-
Reformation? Justify your answer by reference to the evidence in this
chapter.

References

G. Barraclough, *Factors in German History*, Blackwell, 1946
J. Idigoras, 'Censura inédita del padre Francisco Toledo, sobre el catecismo del
    arzobispo Carranza', *Revista Española de Teologia*, XXIX, 1969
P. McNair, *Peter Martyr in Italy: An Anatomy of Apostasy*, Clarendon Press, 1967
H. Oberman, *Luther: Man between God and the Devil*, Yale University Press,
    1989
S. Ozment, *The Reformation in the Cities*, Yale University Press, 1975
M. Phillips, *Erasmus and the Northern Renaissance*, Boydell, 1981

For Cameron, Fenlon, Hall, Jedin and McConica, see *Suggestions for further
reading*.

4 The Council of Trent

'If there is no Council, then woe to England, to Denmark, Sweden and Norway! Where will the apostasy end?' When the great anti-Reformation campaigner Johann Eck wrote that in 1537, belief that a council alone could heal the schism was near-universal.

General councils are assemblies of senior clergy, representing the whole church, at which key doctrinal or other matters are settled in decrees considered binding on all Christians. Instruments of church government, they have usually been summoned only in emergencies and have always been regarded as the best means of reform.

From 1471 all papal candidates swore an oath that, if elected, they would call a council within two years – a promise left unfulfilled by eight successive popes. They also ignored the decree *Frequens* of 1417 that commanded councils to meet every ten years. Of what were these popes afraid? They were worried about further losses of sovereignty – in some states, national churches, semi-independent of Rome, were already a fact. When popes and kings quarrelled, as they did regularly, most were threatened with a council to prune their authority. But secular rulers were only part of the danger. The spectre which so terrified Leo X and Clement VII that neither could contemplate summoning a council to tackle Protestantism was the revival of conciliarism. This theoretical model of church government would have made popes subject to regular councils, have taken away their sovereign power by making them share the governance of the church with the bishops and so would have reduced them to the equivalent of an executive director. Leo and Clement were fighting for their political lives – and the primary enemy was not Martin Luther.

Papal obstinacy was challenged principally by Charles V, who repeatedly urged the need for a council and even threatened to call one himself, as Roman emperors had done a thousand years before. Equally, Charles tried to bully the papacy into issuing the summons, as Emperor Sigismund had done in 1413–15. The emperor was then widely considered to be God's vicar and guardian of the church, the secular counterpart to the pope. Among the laity, therefore, he was in a unique position to influence ecclesiastical affairs.

Yet Charles hesitated to strike the decisive blow. Did he realise just how weak the papacy of the 1520s was? Perhaps too loyal, certainly too deferential, the emperor's forbearance meant that nothing happened until attitudes changed within Rome, and that had to wait upon the election of Paul III in October 1534. Even then, however, there was no immediate resolution, for pope and emperor, united now in wanting a council, were divided over its agenda. While Paul looked primarily to the restoration of doctrinal clarity and papal authority, Charles believed that thorough institutional reform must come first. Only then would Protestants feel able to negotiate a formula for reunion with Rome.

4.1 Papal tactics

Never offer a Council, never refuse it directly. On the contrary, show yourself willing to comply with the request, but stress the difficulties in the way. Thus you will be able to ward it off.

Jerome Aleander, Archbishop of Brindisi, to Clement VII, 1528, in L. von Pastor, *The History of the Popes*, Kegan Paul, Trench Truisner, London, 1923, X, p. 385

4.2 Broken papal promises?

As regards Pope Clement, owing to difficulties of a personal nature,[1] and despite promises made to His Majesty to convoke a council within the space of one year, it was never possible to make him fulfil his commitment. His successor declared at the commencement of his pontificate that he promised to convoke the council immediately, and exhibited a lively desire to provide the remedy for the evils which had befallen Christianity, and for the abuses of the Church. Nevertheless, that first zeal gradually cooled down and, following the steps and example of Clement, he temporised with soft words.

[1] He was illegitimate and so feared deposition.

Autobiography of Charles V, ed. L. Simpson, London, 1862, p. 74

4.3 Imperial procedural considerations

Two remedies only present themselves: the emperor must go to Germany and punish the heretics with severity, or a general council must be convoked. As it is impossible for him to go soon to Germany, he begs the pope to decide what he

ought to do ... As the Germans have asked for a general council to be held in
Germany, it would be well if His Holiness would ... [call] a general council at   5
Trent. The Germans consider Trent as a German city, although it is, properly
speaking, Italian. Although the council ought to be convoked at Trent early next
spring, it can afterwards be transferred to another Italian city (Rome, for
example), or wherever the pope likes.

Charles V to his ambassador in Rome, July 1524, in Kidd, *Documents,*
p. 141

4.4 False dawns

We summoned an ecumenical council of those bishops and fathers whose duty is
to attend, to be opened in Mantua on 23rd May 1537 ... But as the enemy of
mankind always plots against pious enterprises, at the very outset, contrary to our
hopes and expectations, the city of Mantua was refused us ... In the meantime,
the Turk, our cruel and everlasting enemy, having attacked Italy with a powerful   5
fleet, captured, sacked and ravaged several cities on the shores of Apulia ... We
considered it a matter of prime importance both for the celebration of the council
and for Christendom that the Christian princes be united in peace and concord,
and so we did not fail to implore and beseech our most beloved sons in Christ,
Charles, ever august Emperor of the Romans, and Francis, the Most Christian   10
King, the two chief props of the Christian name, to come together in a
conference with us ... [Though] a true and lasting peace between the two princes
could not be effected ... nevertheless a truce of ten years was agreed upon; and
hoping that as a result of this the holy council might be celebrated ... we urged
the princes to come to the council themselves and to bring with them their   15
prelates ... On both these points, however, they excused themselves ... We desired
in our choice of a new place for holding the council to have in mind both the
common welfare of Christendom and the convenience of the German nation, and
seeing that among the various places proposed these desired the city of Trent,
we, though of the opinion that everything could be transacted more conveniently   20
in a cis-Alpine city, nevertheless yielded with paternal charity ... Bishops from
Germany and from the nations bordering on Germany can assemble very early
and those from France, Spain and other more remote provinces without difficulty
... God himself and we can in justice claim particular attendance from the
prelates and princes of Germany, for since it is chiefly on their account and at   25
their wishes that the council has been summoned, and in the very city they
desired.

Initio nostri, **bull of Paul III, May 1542 summoning the Council to open
on 1 November, in** *Canons and Decrees of the Council of Trent,* **ed. H. J.
Schroeder, TAN Books and Publishers Inc., Rockford, 1978, pp. 2–4, 7–9**

Questions

1   Why should it matter where the council met [**4.3, 4.4**]?
2   Explain the meaning in **4.4** of:
    (i)   'ecumenical' [**line 1**]
    (ii) 'the enemy of mankind' [**lines 2–3**]
    (iii) 'cis-Alpine' [**line 21**]
3   Does **4.1** explain papal behaviour in **4.4** and imperial complaints in **4.2**?
4   From your reading, assess the following statements:
    (i)   'A council to settle the Lutheran problem was the last thing France wanted' (Evennett, *The Cardinal of Lorraine and the Council of Trent*, 1930)
    (ii) 'The popes were too Italian, the emperor too Spanish to agree on how to help either Germany or the church' (Hillerbrand, *The Reformation in its own Words*, 1964)

Trent and doctrine

Trent finally opened on 13 December 1545. Paul's bull charged it with 'the uprooting of heresy, the restoring of peace and unity, and the reformation of ecclesiastical discipline and morals'. European power-politics interrupted and shaped its work as much as they had delayed its meeting. The possibility that Trent would be terminated in 1547 or 1552 with its work woefully incomplete was very real. Even in 1560, many a reformer could 'doubt if Catholic reform would ever come to anything' (Schenk, 1950). The Council opened with a mere 29 bishops present, just 5 per cent of the prelates from remaining Catholic territory. Of those attending at any point during its meetings, three-quarters were Italian, and one-tenth Spanish. Until a significant French contingent arrived in 1562, almost none had any first-hand experience of the Reformation crisis. Therein lies the key to understanding Trent's theological approach. Inadequate in representation and ignorant of Reformation realities, it never tried to comprehend the heretics. In opposition to the spirit of Regensburg, Trent took on the mantle of defender of the faith as it built the theological equivalent of the Berlin Wall. Trent replaced medieval doctrinal pluralism with doctrinal certainties.

Salvation theology and authority in the church were its primary concerns, for Protestant attack had made their resolution urgent and, once achieved, Rome would be able to match the heretics' great credal statements of Augsburg (Lutheran, 1530) and Heidelberg (Calvinist, 1563). Trent only ever discussed theological issues disputed by the Protestants, refuting their alternative teachings and reaffirming the Catholic beliefs under attack. Indeed, 'while there had been heresies and schisms before the Reformation, the sheer range of doctrines disputed represented an unprecedented threat' (Pelikan, 1984). By these actions, the Roman church affirmed its teaching authority and declared itself the only infallible judge. At long last, collective action against the Reformation was under way.

4.5 Which Bible, which text?

Not a little advantage will accrue to the church if it be made known which of all the editions of the sacred books now in circulation is to be regarded as authentic ... [The Council] ordains that the old Latin Vulgate edition which, in use for so many years, has been approved by the Church, be in public lectures, disputations, sermons and expositions held as authentic, and that no one dare or presume   5
under any pretext to reject it.

Decree of April 1546, in Schroeder, *Canons and Decrees*, p. 18

4.6 Justification

When the Apostle says that man is justified by faith and freely, these words are to be understood in that sense in which the uninterrupted unanimity of the Catholic Church has held and expressed them, namely, that faith is the beginning of human salvation ... [The decree ended with canons listing 33 errors to be condemned:]   5
   1. That man can be justified before God by his own works, whether done either by his own natural powers or through the teaching of the law, without divine grace through Jesus Christ ...
   4. That the man's free will, moved and aroused by God, by assenting to God's call and action in no way co-operates toward disposing and preparing itself to   10
obtain the grace of justification, that it cannot refuse its assent if it wishes, but that, as some inanimate thing, it does nothing ...
   7. That all works done before justification ... are truly sins or merit the hatred of God; that the more earnestly one strives to dispose himself to grace, the more grievously he sins ...   15
   9. That the sinner is justified by faith alone, meaning that nothing else is required ... [and] it is not in any way necessary that he be prepared and disposed by the action of his own will ...
   11. That men are justified by the sole imputation of the justice of Christ ...
   24. That justice received is not preserved and also not increased before God   20
through good works, but that those works are merely fruits and signs of justification obtained, not the cause of its increase ...
   30. That after the reception of the grace of justification the guilt is so remitted

and the debt of eternal punishment so blotted out ... that no debt of temporal
punishment remains to be discharged ... before the gates of heaven can be   25
opened ...

**Decree and canons of January 1547, in Schroeder, *Canons and Decrees*,
pp. 34–5, 43, 45, 46**

4.7   The Tridentine Creed

I profess that true God is offered in the Mass, a proper, propitiatory sacrifice for
the living and the dead, and that in the Holy Eucharist there are truly and
substantially the body and blood, together with the soul and the divinity of Our
Lord Jesus Christ, and that conversion is made of the whole substance of bread
into his body and of the whole substance of wine into his blood, which   5
conversion the Catholic Church calls transubstantiation. I also confess that the
whole and entire Christ and the true sacrament is taken under the one species
alone.

I hold unswervingly that there is a purgatory and that the souls there detained
are helped by the intercessions of the faithful. Likewise also that the Saints who   10
reign with Christ are to be venerated and invoked; that they offer prayers to God
for us and that their relics are to be venerated ... I affirm that the power of
indulgences has been left by Christ in the Church, and that their use is very
salutary for Christian people.

I recognise the Holy Catholic and Apostolic Roman Church as the Mother and   15
Mistress of all churches; and I vow and swear true obedience to the Roman
Pontiff, successor of Blessed Peter, Chief of the Apostles, and representative of
Jesus Christ.

**From *Injunction nobis*, bull of Pius IV, November 1564, in Kidd,
Documents, pp. 357–8†**

4.8   Regrets at what might have been

Oh that those for whose sake this voyage was chiefly undertaken had decided to
board it with us; that those who caused us to take up this work in hand had
participated in the erection of this edifice! Then indeed we would now have
reason for greater rejoicing. But it is certainly not through our fault that it so
happened. For that reason, we chose this city, situated at the entrance to   5
Germany ... For a long time we awaited them and never did we cease to exhort
them to come here and learn the truth.

**Jerome Ragazonius, Bishop of Famagusta, preaching to the final
Tridentine meeting, December 1563, in Schroeder, *Canons and Decrees*,
p. 259**

Questions

1 'If we abandon the scholastic tradition for the ways of Erasmus and Lefèvre, none will be more delighted than the heretics' (Domingo de Soto, Dominican delegate at Trent, 1546). Explain the difference between Humanist and Tridentine appeals to the biblical text [2.2–2.4, **4.5**].

2 With reference to **4.6** and from the table on page 18 explain:
   (i) the heresy condemned by canon 1. Did the canon also condemn medieval Catholic practice?
   (ii) why these canons were necessary
   (iii) why this decree resulted from genuine debate, whereas Tridentine doctrine mostly repeated old decrees from ancient councils and popes.

3 (i) Explain why **4.7** (paragraph 1) is Catholic, not Protestant.
   (ii) What purpose does the last sentence of paragraph 1 serve?
   (iii) How does **4.7** reflect the teaching of **4.6** (canon 30)?

4 'Nothing, not even Scripture, is authentic without the authority of the Church' (Cardinal Sadoleto, 1539). Why did the question of authority assume central importance?

5 Does the attitude of Ragazonius in **4.8** explain why his dream remained unfulfilled? Explain your answer.

Trent and church reform

This section examines the twin emphases of Tridentine reform: the pastoral mission of the clergy to the people and the supervisory role of bishops in seeing that it was carried out. As doctrine preoccupied the first two Tridentine sessions (1545–7, 1551–2), pastoral and disciplinary reform dominated the third (1562–3). To the bishops at Trent, 'reform of the church' meant the overhaul of structures at the diocesan and parochial levels. Only then could there be spiritual and moral reform among the people. The clergy were to be the instruments of renewal. But it nearly did not happen. Within papal circles, reform had fallen under suspicion. These were the years of the *zelanti*, hawkish zealots led by Cardinal Carafa, the erstwhile reformer who founded the Roman Inquisition (1542) and who as Pope Paul IV (1555–9) ruled with an austere fanaticism shot through with more than a hint of paranoia. Repression was the order of the day. By 1562, however, the situation had been transformed. The arrival of French bishops anxious for wholesale reform to check advancing Calvinism cannot explain everything: France had no more influence over Rome than had Charles V. Rather, the change reflected new Catholic self-confidence. At the very moment Trent was sorting out doctrine and Jesuit missions were yielding their first fruits, Lutheranism faltered: Luther's death (1546) robbed the movement of its great dynamic, theological schism split his disciples, and the Peace of Augsburg (1555) halted their German expansion. Meanwhile, the papacy too had changed. All nine popes elected between 1559 and 1600 were committed reformers. As Paul III had foreseen when promoting *spirituali*, new-style cardinals would produce new-style popes.

4.9   Reform postponed

The council was suspended[1] on Good Friday and it seemed that I saw before me the body of Christ (of which the Council, representing the whole Church, is an image). So recently, the Council had raised the brightest hopes of reform. Now, like Our Lord on his passion day, it seemed scourged with rods, dead and ready for burial. But that same day, I was reminded of Christ's resurrection and all the   5
blessings which followed. Then did I conceive new hope.

[1] Following the renewal of the Habsburg–Valois war and rumours that Trent would be attacked.

Cardinal Pole to Cardinal Seripando, July 1552, in *Epistolae Reginaldi Poli Cardinalis*, ed. A. Quirini, Brescia, 1744, IV, pp. 71–2†

4.10   Towards a quality clergy

1. Since by divine law it is enjoined on all to whom is entrusted the cure of souls to know their sheep, to offer sacrifice for them and to feed them by preaching the divine word, by administering the sacraments ... to exercise a fatherly care in behalf of the poor and other distressed persons and to apply themselves to all other pastoral duties, all of which cannot be rendered and fulfilled by those who   5
do not watch over and are not with their flock, but desert it after the manner of hirelings, the council admonishes and exhorts them ... that the period of absence in a single year, continuous or interrupted, ought in no case to exceed two or at the most three months.
   7. All who wish to dedicate themselves to the sacred ministry shall be   10
summoned for the Wednesday before ordination ... [when] the bishop shall carefully investigate and examine the parentage, person, age, education, morals, learning and faith of those who are to be ordained.
   12. No one shall in future be promoted ... to deacon before the twenty-third, and to the priesthood before the twenty-fifth year of his age. However, the   15
bishop should know that not all who have attained that age are to be admitted to these orders, but only those who are worthy ...
   14. [Those] ... accepted for the order of priesthood shall have a good

testimonial ... [and] have served in the office of deacon for one entire year ... and
[be] so conspicuous for piety and purity of morals that a shining example of good   20
works and a guidance for good living may be expected. The bishop shall see to it
that they celebrate mass at least on the Lord's days and on solemn festivals ...

17. [On] all persons by whatever title distinguished, even though of the
cardinalate, one ecclesiastical benefice only shall be conferred. If that is not
sufficient to provide him on whom it is conferred with a decent livelihood, then   25
it is permissible to confer on him another simple benefice that will afford a
sufficiency, provided both do not require personal residence ... Those who now
hold several parochial churches, or one cathedral and one parochial church, shall
be strictly bound, all dispensations and unions for life notwithstanding, retaining
one only ... to resign all others within a period of six months.[1]

[1] This decree repeated one of 1179. Trent forbade pluralism of bishoprics in 1547.

**Reform decrees of July and (no. 17) November 1563, in Schroeder, *Canons
and Decrees*, pp. 164–5, 169, 171–3, 207**

4.11   Diocesan seminaries

Since the age of youth, unless rightly trained, is inclined to follow after the
pleasure of the world, and unless educated from its tender years in piety and
religion before the habits of vice take possession of the whole man, will never
perfectly ... persevere in ecclesiastical discipline, the Council decrees that all
cathedral churches shall be bound, each according to its means and the extent of   5
its diocese, to provide for, to educate in religion, and to train in ecclesiastical
discipline, a certain number of boys of their city and diocese ... in a college ...
Into this college shall be received such as are at least twelve years of age, born of
lawful wedlock, who know how to read and write competently, and whose
character and inclination justify the hope that they will dedicate themselves   10
forever to the ecclesiastical ministry ... That they may be the better trained, they
shall forthwith and always wear the tonsure and the clerical garb; they shall study
grammar, singing ... Sacred Scripture, ecclesiastical books, the homilies [lives] of
the saints, the manner of administering the sacraments, especially those things
that seem adapted to the hearing of confessions, and the rites and ceremonies.   15
The bishop shall see that they are present every day at the sacrifice of the mass
[and] confess their sins at least once a month ... All these and other things
beneficial and needful for this purpose each bishop shall make it their duty by
frequent visitation to see always observed. The disobedient and incorrigible, and
the disseminators of depraved morals they shall punish severely, even with   20
expulsion ... And if the prelates should prove negligent in the erection of the
seminary and its maintenance, it shall be the duty of the archbishop to rebuke the
bishop sharply and compel him to comply.

Reform decree of July 1563, in Schroeder, *Canons and Decrees*, pp. 175–8

4.12   The duties of a bishop

2. Provincial synods, wherever they have been omitted, shall be restored for the regulation of morals, the correction of abuses, the settlement of controversies ... Wherefore archbishops in person shall not neglect to convoke a synod within a year at least from the termination of the present Council and after that at least every third year ... [All clergy] shall be absolutely bound to attend.   5

   3. [Archbishops and bishops] shall not neglect to visit their respective dioceses, either personally or, if they are lawfully hindered, through their vicar-general; if by reason of its extent they are unable to make a visitation of the whole annually, they shall ... visit at least the greater part of it, so that the whole may be completed in two years ... The chief purpose of all these visitations shall be, after   10 the extirpation of heresies, to restore sound doctrine, to guard good morals and to correct such as are evil, to animate the people by exhortations with religion, peace and innocence ...

   4. Desiring that the office of preaching, which belongs chiefly to the bishops, be exercised as often as possible for the welfare of the faithful ... [bishops] shall   15 personally, each in his own church, announce the Sacred Scriptures and the divine law or, if lawfully hindered, have it done by those whom they shall appoint ... but in other churches, by the parish priest ... And this they shall do at least on all Sundays and solemn festival days, but during the season of the feasts of Lent and Advent, daily, or at least on three days of the week ... The bishop   20 shall [also] ... see to it that, at least on Sundays and other festival days, the children of every parish be carefully taught the rudiments of the faith.

   7. That the faithful may approach the sacraments with greater reverence and devotion of mind, the Council commands all bishops ... when they are about to administer them to the people, they shall first, in a manner adapted to the mental   25 ability of those who receive them, explain their efficacy and use, but also they shall see to it that the same is done piously and prudently by every parish priest, and in the vernacular tongue if need be and if it can be done conveniently, in accordance with the form which will be prescribed ... by the Council in a catechism, which the bishops shall have faithfully translated into the language of   30 the people.

Reform decree of November 1563, in Schroeder, *Canons and Decrees,* **pp. 192–7**

Questions

1   Why should **4.9** help us to judge Trent correctly?
2   Explain the meaning of:
   (i)   'the cure of souls' [**4.10 line 1**]
   (ii)   'to offer sacrifice for them' [**4.10 line 2**]; read the table on page 18
      before you answer

   (iii) 'ordination' [**4.10 line 11**]
   (iv) 'a catechism' [**4.12 line 30**]
3 How far do **4.10–4.12** confirm the view that 'the salvation of souls
   was the decisive criterion for Tridentine reform' (Jedin, *A History of the
   Council of Trent*, 1957)?
4 What do **4.10** and **4.12** reveal about Trent's concept of bishops?
5 'Though slow to be implemented, no proposal of Trent was to exert
   more crucial effects than the establishing of seminaries' (Dickens, *The
   Counter Reformation*, 1968). Suggest reasons why **4.11** was so significant.

Unfinished business?

Tridentine debates could be turbulent and none was more stormy than the
row which flared up in 1562 over episcopal residence: must bishops live in
their dioceses and simultaneously hold no other positions? When so many
regarded church posts as pieces of property and financial assets for their
family, considerable opposition was guaranteed. At stake was, however, a far
greater issue. If bishops derived their authority directly from Christ by
divine command, popes could not grant them leave of absence. Powerful
voices, mostly Spanish and French, were raised against papal dispensing
power and in favour of greater independence for bishops. Here was another
of those fundamental issues which medieval theologians and administrators
had failed to resolve. Had Jesus committed jurisdiction and government to
St Peter alone or to all twelve apostles equally? Was the position of the pope
just a primacy of honour? Both sides appealed to the Fathers, especially St
Cyprian (d. AD 258). Debate was so heated that punches were even thrown.
The vote in April on whether episcopal residence was a divine obligation
offered no obvious way out: 'yes' 67, 'no' 38, 'the pope should decide' 34.
After much lobbying, Cardinal Morone, the presiding papal legate, secured
approval for a statement that bishops were the successors of the apostles and
instituted by the Holy Spirit to rule the church. Ambiguity alone won its
acceptance and, at the same time, neutralised it. Pius IV had been lucky, and
he knew it. Trent was never therefore permitted to debate the position and
authority of the papacy, even though both had been subjected to violent
Protestant attack. For all the fears of popes before Paul III, papal prerogatives emerged untouched and were soon being strengthened. After all, this
was the era of absolutist monarchies.

4.13   Tridentine opinions on episcopal authority

4.13(a)

Bishops are instituted by divine right, by Christ ... If the pope alone has authority from Christ, and that authority alone is by divine right because he alone is instituted by Christ, then the pope is the only bishop appointed by the authority of God. That cannot be for, as Cyprian says, 'The office of bishop is sacred, held individually by the gift of God.'

The Archbishop of Granada, 13 October 1562

4.13(b)

We have it on the unanimous authority of the Fathers that bishops were instituted by Christ. Since their authority is thus held by divine right, so therefore is the government of their diocese. Cyprian makes clear that Christ chose, appointed and gave authority to all the Apostles, not just Peter. To all Christ gave power to forgive sin. To all Christ gave responsibility for the care of   5
his flock. As all the Apostles were equal and identical in power so all bishops are equal and identical in power, and each bishop in his diocese is the equal of the pope ... Authority derives not from the pope, but from Christ. The pope is a channel of that authority, not its source.

The Bishop of Auria, 19 November 1562

4.13(c)

While it is true that the Apostles received their authority immediately from Christ, it is equally true that bishops, although successors of the Apostles, receive their authority through the pope and from him derive their jurisdiction. Order and jurisdiction are separate parts of their office. Cyprian refers only to the order, the rank of bishop, as being instituted by Christ. Cyprian does not state that   5
government of the church was entrusted by Christ to all the Apostles. Rather, Cyprian is clear that the keys of power and authority were entrusted to Peter alone ... [and] describes bishops as 'springing from the papacy as from a fount'.

The Bishop of Cava, 5 November 1562

4.13(d)

Heresy begins when men turn to listen to their own fancies, rather than follow the narrow way. And what is that way? It is the way of Christ and of his chosen Apostle ... Only one bishop and judge may sit in Christ's place. All who abandon the throne of Peter abandon the foundation stone of the church. Only in the

supremacy of that throne is the church held in the unity of the seamless robe of   5
Christ. How can that unity, which comes from God, be split among a thousand
different voices?

The Cistercian Abbot-General, 7 December 1562

All extracts from *Consilium Tridentium, Diariorum, Actorum Nova
Collectio*, Freiburg, 1901, IX p. 50, II pp. 733–5, IX pp. 126, 129, II p. 662
respectively†

Questions

1   Are **4.13(a)** and **4.13(b)** in agreement? Justify your answer.
2   (a)   Explain the consequences if Trent accepted **4.13(a)** and **4.13(b)**
            rather than **4.13(c)** and **4.13(d)**.
      (b)   Does **4.10** reflect any of the opinions in **4.13(a)–(d)**?
      (c)   Suggest reasons why the appeal to history was so crucial.
3   Do the divisions represented in **4.13(a)–(d)** alter your view of the stance
      taken against Luther [3.1]? Explain your answer.
4   From your wider reading, explain why the kings of France and Spain
      encouraged their bishops to support **4.13(a)** and **4.13(b)**. Read Chapter
      8 (pages 154–157) before you answer.

Summary

How helpful are the following statements in judging the Council of Trent?
   (i)   'Luther was responsible for the calling of the Council' (Bainton,
            Studies on the Reformation, 1964)
  (ii)   'Henceforth, religious orthodoxy would be defined as a narrow
            gate through which few truths passed' (O'Malley, *The First Jesuits*,
            1993)
 (iii)   'It did not work a revolution in the church order or rid it of all
            the abuses that encumbered it, but it did affirm what it believed to
            be the truths of the faith and it took steps against some of the
            most salient defects and deficiencies' (Olin, *Catholic Reform from
            Ximenes to Trent*, 1990)
 (iv)   'The principal accomplishments of the council did not lie in
            dogmatic formulations, but in legislation regarding the reform and
            administration of the church' (Pelikan, *The Christian Tradition:
            Reformation of Church and Dogma, 1300–1700*, 1984)

References

R. Bainton, *Studies on the Reformation*, Hodder, 1964

A. Dickens, *The Counter Reformation*, Thames and Hudson, 1968

H. Evennett, *The Cardinal of Lorraine and the Council of Trent*, Cambridge University Press, 1930

H. Hillerbrand, *The Reformation in its own Words*, SCM Press, 1964

W. Schenk, *Reginald Pole, Cardinal of England*, Longman, 1950

For Jedin, Olin, O'Malley (1993) and Pelikan, see *Suggestions for further reading*.

5 Structural reform

As the Council of Trent prepared to disperse, the Polish cardinal Stanilaus Hosius (Bishop of Ermland, d. 1579) reminded his fellow delegates that 'whether or not those souls held by the heretics are lost, we must ensure that, for the benefit of the souls we still hold and for which we as priests shall be answerable to God, the church be renewed.' Chapters 5 to 7 examine responses to that challenge, Chapter 5 dealing with structures and institutions, Chapters 6 and 7 with the relationship between church and people. Was a new Catholicism created? Old-style pro-Catholic history had no doubts in ascribing to Trent responsibility for a swift, successful transformation of the Catholic position. Established habits do not, however, die easily. Reform is rarely popular. As these chapters assess post-Tridentine Catholicism, the true significance of the Council is itself under scrutiny.

The development of a papal monarchy

Papal monarchy meant two different things: rule over the church and rule over the papal states. During the century before Trent, they were seriously out of balance. Popes thought and behaved as mere Italian princes, carving out a temporal dominion to permit them political and financial independence. Only with Julius III (elected 1550) did they begin once again to act as if they possessed the universal spiritual leadership they claimed. Theologians spent much ink providing the theoretical basis for a 'new, systematic and self-consciously orthodox view of the papacy' (Hamilton, 1963). In a strict sense, Tridentine decree had nothing to do with it for, as we saw in Chapter 4, the papacy managed to exempt itself from examination. But the vigorous overhaul of papal government did not develop in isolation. Improvements in diocesan administration, some pre-dating Trent, were setting a new standard. So too were secular bureaucratic developments, themselves in part driven by a marked contemporary desire for efficiency. The muddle that had been the medieval papal machine (administrative, judicial, financial) was rationalised by an on-going initiative, launched by Paul III (elected 1534) and concluded largely by Sixtus V (d. 1590), to create a sophisticated central bureaucracy second to none in Europe. Some organs of government were re-ordered while others were new creations. Most notable was the series of spe-cialist committees, known as congregations, formally constituted by Sixtus in 1588. Rapidly, these became the centre of gravity for church government and gave the papacy a power of dealing efficiently, systematically and reasonably swiftly with a burgeoning mountain of paperwork.

A confident and supreme papal monarchy quickly emerged. Medieval constitutional speculation about whether there was a balance of power with-in the hierarchy, or whether supreme authority was vested in the whole body of the Christian faithful, was not answered. It was simply brushed aside. Papal authority had been so attacked that the needs and demands of Catholic recovery encouraged strong executive power. Once again, the Catholic church set the political pace. As the papacy had forged concepts of sover-eignty and centralisation for medieval Europe so now it 'provided the prototype of the secular sovereign state, a single society under a sovereign head' (Prodi, 1987). It is no accident that the concept of papal infallibility, invented in the late 13th century but long thought 'a pestiferous novelty' (John XXII, 1324), now became prominent in Catholic thinking. As the new–model papacy took command, internal disorder and opposition were checked. The often unruly college of cardinals, which 'stood to the pope very much as a turbulent and obstructive baronage to a medieval king' (Evennett, 1968) was thoroughly tamed, in personal lifestyle as much as in authority. No longer would they claim a share in papal power or see themselves as a representative international senate. Instead, they had by 1500 become almost exclusively Italian and by 1600 were submissive servants transacting the pope's business, 'a docile group of individuals living only in the reflected light of the pope' (Antonovics, 1972).

Do not forget the context in which this was happening. Late medieval popes had surrendered considerable control over church affairs to individual secular rulers. They did so in order to neutralise the threat that 15th-century conciliar theory posed to their own monarchical position. But 'the alliance with royalism was itself not without dangers to the papacy' (Black, 1970). Outside the papal states, reformist popes could consolidate only what remained to them and, as Chapter 8 shows, Catholic princes were by no means prepared to give Rome a free hand. The papacy had been forced into the role of a junior partner. Further, this was the era when the image of rulers was first composed and packaged to real effect. Building projects and every kind of spectacle were used to display the authority and mission of the Roman church, the papal office and individual popes. How efficient the new administration actually proved still remains to be determined by scholars. Control of officials was then a notorious problem in all governments. The sale of offices reached its peak under the greatest of bureaucratic reformers, Sixtus V. When symbolism was so blatantly manipulated by regimes, we must be careful not to let illusion of power pass for reality.

5.1 The papacy: what Trent actually said

(i) The holy Council declares that each and all things which under whatever causes and words have been established ... have been so decreed that in these matters the authority of the Apostolic See is and is understood to be intact.

'On the authority of the Apostolic See', December 1563

(ii) The holy Council commands patriarchs, primates, archbishops, bishops and all others who by right or custom ought to be present at the provincial synod, that in the very first synod to be held after the close of the present Council ... they all do promise and profess true obedience to the supreme Roman Pontiff.

'By whom the Decrees are to be taught', December 1563

(iii) The holy Council trusts that the most blessed Roman Pontiff will see the necessities of the provinces be provided for by summoning ... persons he shall judge competent to discuss matters, or by the celebration of a general council if he should deem it necessary, or in any other way as shall seem to him more suitable.

'Concerning the acceptance and observation of the Decrees', December 1563

(iv) [The Council's legates] do humbly petition in the name of the Ecumenical Council that Your Holiness deign to confirm each and all of the things that have been decreed.

'Petition for confirmation of the conciliar decrees', January 1564

All in Schroeder, *Canons and Decrees*, pp. 253, 233–4, 256, 268

5.2 A papal conspiracy?

The popes, fearing precisely lest the council should show them in their true colour, and seek to recall them to a sense of their duty, have, by diabolical instigation, taken no notice of the ancient councils and stultified the recent ones to the holding of which they have been compelled to consent, for by trickery and

intimidation they brought it about that this assembly was not only unable to   5
investigate the truth, but were even compelled to exalt still further the worldly
power of the papacy and to destroy the last vestiges of the church's liberty.

Paolo Sarpi, a Servite friar, *A History of the Council of Trent,* **London,
1619, p. 2**

5.3   Papal supremacy

5.3(a)

As a commonwealth can have only one head, and the Church is no less a visible
assembly than the kingdom of France or the republic of Venice, so is the pope
that single head who guides, instructs, interprets and corrects ... Supreme
authority in matters of faith and morals, jurisdiction and lawmaking rest with him
alone. That is why only the pope can summon a general council and the decisions   5
of such a body require his specific confirmation before they have any validity.

5.3(b)

The union of spiritual and temporal responsibility for the Patrimony of St Peter[1]
in the papal person promotes greater unity and peace within Christendom, brings
temporal rulers closer to the one spiritual prince, encourages respect for His
Holiness, provides the resources which enable him to throw back infidels and
heretics. In short, Christendom is blessed and preserved through the papal   5
lordship over the States of the Church.[1]

[1] Both terms for the papal states.

Francisco Suarez, Jesuit professor of theology: 5.3(a) *A Defence of the
Catholic and Apostolic Faith* **(1613); 5.3(b)** *A Treatise on the Laws and on
God the Lawgiver* **(1612), Naples, 1872, I, pp. 307, 129†**

Questions

1   (a) How did Trent see the relationship between council and pope
        [5.1]?
    (b) In what ways did that reflect the debate on episcopal residence
        [4.13]?
2   (a) What does Sarpi allege in **5.2**?
    (b) What can you find out about Sarpi to explain his hostility?
    (c) Can we trust his *History*? Explain your answer.
3   From **5.3(a)** and **5.3(b)**, summarise the justifications for papal monarchy.
4   Comment on the image of Catholic Christendom painted by **5.3(b)**.

5.4   Structural change: congregations and consistories

5.4(a)

The Architect of all things has united His creatures together in such a way,
sweetly assigning to each its special purpose, that all serve and complete each
other ... He has divided the body of the Church militant, which is an image of
the Church triumphant, into its various members, which, united to their head
and joined together by the bond of charity, help each other reciprocally, in such a   5
way that the health and preservation of the whole body depends upon this.

    Therefore, with good reason, the Roman Pontiff, whom Jesus Christ has
appointed as the visible head of His body, which is the Church, and Who wills
that he should guide and rule all the churches, surrounds himself by many
assistants for so immense a burden, and sets them by his side, whether they be   10
the venerable bishops whom he sends throughout the world to care for the
scattered flocks, or the exalted body of Cardinals who, as the most noble
members in immediate relation with the head, the Supreme Pontiff, as were the
Apostles with Jesus Christ, are ever by his side, and are his first associates and
fellow labourers in work and counsel, to the end that he himself, by sharing with   15
them and the other officers of the Roman Curia the gigantic burden of anxiety
and business, may not, with the assistance of divine grace, succumb. Moved,
therefore, by the example of the great Moses, who ... by the order of God set up
the senate of the seventy elders, that they might with him bear the burden of the
people, and that he alone might not be troubled by them, we have decided to   20
share the pontifical burden, which would be formidable for the shoulders of the
angels themselves, among the senators of the world, our brethren the Cardinals ...
That they may more easily and speedily discharge their business, that they may
find various assemblies and congregations of Cardinals, ready to deal with definite
questions and business, and in order that the Cardinals themselves may more   25
easily fulfil the task assigned to them, administer their charge more diligently,
and counsel us more suitably, and finally, in order that there may never be a lack
of men in high position, well versed in public affairs, we have therefore set up
fifteen congregations, drawn from the Sacred College, and to each we have
assigned definite business, in such a way that in more important and difficult   30
questions they may have recourse to us, while to each we have given the
necessary faculties and authority.

Immensa Dei, **bull of Sixtus V, January 1588, in Pastor,** *History of the*
Popes, **XXI, Routledge pp. 247–9**

5.4(b)

The entire temporal and spiritual government is at the present moment very
different from what it was in the past, because in other times they advised on
great matters of State, and all the rest, in consistories with the cardinals,

otherwise they committed the affairs to the congregations of cardinals because
they would decide what seemed best to them; but now the consistories are used   5
for nothing other than communicating with the collation of the churches and
making public the resolutions of every kind made by the Pope; and the
congregations, from that of the Inquisition – which is maintained with decorum
and reduced every week – to all the others, even that of the Regulars and of the
Bishops, are mere appearance; because, even though they work it out in one way,   10
the Pope does it in another; and as to the most important things ... he never
consults anyone.

**The Venetian ambassador in Rome, 1598, in P. Prodi, *The Papal Prince:
Papal Monarchy in Early Modern Europe*, Cambridge University Press,
1987, p. 87**

5.5   Pope and cardinals: an altered balance of power

5.5(a)

This court is dominated by a 'mixed' prince, since as well as being an ecclesiastic
he also enjoys a great state in the temporal life and because of one of these
elements he then makes himself arbiter of all, and thus it is necessary to see to it
that no prince, either temporal or spiritual, opposes him. In time past, the pope
governed this ecclesiastical monarchy together with the cardinals, and those   5
cardinals had to be satisfied just as the pope himself, because they took part in all
government; now all is changed, and only the pope governs, and the cardinals are
left with nothing but appearances.

Instructions for the Spanish ambassador in Rome, 1580–1

5.5(b)

The pope rules the entire ecclesiastical state with supreme authority and with pure
and absolute imperiousness, and everything depends upon his single desire. So
that truly it can be said to be a royal government, and of a kind most free from
other obligations and ties of law and particular regulations, to which the different
royal states are perhaps subject through the great authority which councils, parlia-   5
ments, barons or populace hold over them ... But the pope with great and absolute
authority orders and grants every matter, without using any other counsel, unless
he wishes to, nor does he receive any hindrance from any contrary constitution ...
The cardinals used to be made participants by the popes in the greatest transac-
tions which took place in that government, which they dealt with by voting in   10
consistory, taking decisions ... But already for some years, that is, during the
pontificate of Pius II [1458–64] up till now, this restriction has progressed so far

that ... the College does not discuss any public transaction, nor does it receive the notices which are sent daily by the ministers of the Apostolic See resident with princes, except rarely ... Even if the pope communicates some of his thought to   15 the College, he does so rather to inform them than to ask for advice. Should he perhaps at some time seek it, or rather look as if he is seeking it, there is seldom anyone who dares to proffer anything but praise of the pope's proposals, trying to flatter rather than to advise ... Each of the cardinals is desirous every day to earn thanks for himself and ... no one wishes to damage himself by opposition.

The Venetian ambassador in Rome, 1595. Both in Prodi, *The Papal Prince*, pp. 218, 37, 81

5.6   Cardinals: reformed characters?

At any rate in public cardinals now stand aloof from every kind of amusement. They are no longer seen riding or driving masked in the company of ladies ... Banquets, games, hunting parties, liveries and all forms of external luxury are all the more at an end because there are no longer any lay persons of high rank at the court, such as were formerly to be found there in great numbers among the   5 relatives and intimates of the pope.

The Venetian ambassador in Rome, 1565, in Pastor, *History of the Popes*, XVI, pp. 79–80

5.7   Papal monarchy and sabotage of Trent?

5.7(a)

The legates and vice-legates[1] claim to be vicars-general of Your Holiness, and therefore proceed in every case against the priests without distinction, whether they are defendants or witnesses, having them arrested, even in their own churches, by the police, who lead them tied like dogs through the public streets of the city and surrounding country and through the piazzas, in the greatest   5 contempt for the clerical habit and for archiepiscopal jurisdiction, and to universal scandal and great damage for the souls, the care of which is impossible to provide, all this taking place without the ordinary[2] knowing. Furthermore, when it happens that some defaulter of the Court seeks asylum in the churches, they seize him there, contravening the bull of ecclesiastical immunity ... a bad   10 example to the princes of the surrounding states by whom, it seems, the clergy are treated better ...

   Although each year they appoint the synodal judges in the diocesan synod, to whom in conformity with the sacred Council of Trent the appeals of the ecclesiastical cases have to be committed, yet they always commit them to their   15 own judges, or to some of the judges of the rota who are mere laymen ... which results in a greater expense for the litigants and small reputation for clerical jurisdiction.

   They also claim authority in the monasteries of nuns, sometimes placing in them married women or widows, because of lawsuits, without the participation of   20
the ordinary, which results in much confusion ... And, besides, they give permission to have fairs and markets against the archiepiscopal edicts and to work on feastdays, when they are asked for, allowing games in the piazzas and public ways on feastdays by tumblers and comedians, while divine offices are being said, and greatly disturbing these. They have orders, proclamations, warnings and   25
summonses read and posted up in the churches and sacristies; matters which are against divine worship and prejudicial to ecclesiastical jurisdiction, which then remains scorned.

¹ The papal states were divided into five legations, governed by cardinals.
² 'the ordinary' = the local bishop.

The Archbishop of Bologna to Clement VIII, November 1598

5.7(b)

If this case does not touch the heart of Your Lordship, and does not obtain from Our Lord permission so that I can exercise my office with the necessary dignity, and in a clear way so that every day I do not have to argue, and therefore my reasons are esteemed so low without my being able to understand the reason. I do not know what to do.

The Bishop of Bologna to Cardinal Ormaneto, July 1569 (Bologna became an archbishopric in 1583). Both in Prodi, *The Papal Prince*, pp. 154–5, 141

Questions

1   Explain the meaning of:
   (i)   'the Church militant' **[5.4(a) line 3]**
   (ii) 'the Roman Curia' **[5.4(a) line 16]**
   (iii) 'temporal and spiritual government' **[5.4(b) line 1]**
2   (a)   From **5.4(a)**, explain the purpose of congregations.
    (b)   From **5.4(b)** and **5.5(b)**, explain the function of consistories.
    (c)   According to **5.4(b)** and **5.5(b)**, why have consistories become irrelevant?
3   (a)   How does **5.4(a)** envisage the relationship between pope and cardinals?
    (b)   How different is the reality as seen by **5.4(b)**, **5.5(a)** and **5.5(b)**?

(c)   Had **4.13(a)** and **4.13(b)** been approved, how different might that
        relationship have been?

4   What impression do **5.5(b)** and **5.6** give of post-Tridentine cardinals?

5   'Rome had ceased to be the licentious city at which Savonarola and
        Luther hurled their anathemas' (Delumeau, *Catholicism between Luther
        and Voltaire*, 1977). Why are **2.20** and **5.5(b)** valuable when assessing
        the speed of that transformation?

6   'Resident bishops suffer many impediments and disturbances from the
        papal governors' (St Carlo Borromeo, Archbishop of Milan, 1569).
        (i)   Of what did Bologna complain in **5.7(a)** and **5.7(b)**?
        (ii)   How revealing do you judge Bologna's reference in **5.7(b)** to his
                'necessary dignity' **[line 2]**?
        (iii) Read **8.24** and then **5.7(a)** and **5.7(b)**. How do you think Philip II
                would have replied had he read both these extracts?

Religious orders

Monasticism could have been the great casualty of 16th-century religious
history. Monasteries in 1500 were far from being the sinks of iniquity often
suggested, but few found them inspiring and many believed they had
outlived their purpose – a view dangerously reinforced after 1517 by the
very high proportion of former monks and friars among Protestant leaders
and clergy. The stirrings of monastic revival were under way before Trent,
but reformist initiatives then were sporadic and often a question of good
intentions. Further, discussion at the Council was so minimal and very last-
minute that only 'a skeleton law' (Jedin, 1980) was produced. St Ignatius did
exceedingly well to secure papal approval for a new order in 1540. The tide
was still running against the religious.

If you visit France, Germany or Central Europe today you will find, however, a prodigious number of abbeys built or rebuilt in the 17th and 18th
centuries. They bear witness to a remarkable recovery of vitality, of commitment and of popularity, as does the dominant role which orders took in
colonial missionary work. New orders were created and old ones were reborn
across those centuries: the reformed Cistercians known as Trappists began
in 1662, the new Brothers of the Christian Schools not until 1688. Two particular characteristics mark this great era in monastic history: contemplative
prayer within the cloister and social action outside in the surrounding
streets. 'Activism in grace' guided the new orders. Piety and charity were
inseparable to a Christianity fully engaged with the world. Something of that
new creativity can be seen in the experiences of the Savoyard bishop St

Francis de Sales (d. 1622) and the Spanish nun St Teresa of Avila (d. 1582), two very different reformers of female orders. But before examining their ambitions, some of the formidable problems facing all who would refine monasticism must be considered.

5.8 Monastic reform: structural difficulties

Any ordinary remedy would be useless. To succeed, we need a reformer of great authority and prudence with ample powers ... I say not only ample, but absolute and without appeal, for the monks are very experienced and clever in chicanery ... I think it would be right in the case of certain monasteries to introduce religious of a different congregation, such as the Feuillants[1] or the Carthusians ...   5
Here is my reason. Since some of the monasteries are subject to unreformed superiors, the reform, even if accepted by the community, would not last.
How could superiors maintain discipline and reform in dependencies when their mothers do not even know what reform is? ... As for the others ... these will have to be secularised since the monks are Canons Regular of Saint Augustine,   10
but belonging to a congregation which has no General, no Provincial, no Chapter, no Visitor, no express form of vow, no Rule, no Constitutions.

[1] 'Feuillants' = reformed Cistercians, founded 1577.

Francis de Sales, Bishop of Geneva to the papal nuncio, December 1603, in *Œuvres de St François de Sales*, Annecy, 1892, XII, pp. 239–43†

5.9 Monastic reform: problems with personnel

5.9(a)

The whole state was full of renegade monks ... [When] I tried to take measures against this abuse, it turned out that they enjoyed innumerable, far-reaching favours from various noblemen and senators whom they served, as tutors or in other capacities ... The officers and prelates of religious orders on various pretexts refuse to take them in. Some of them plead poverty, others the great   5
number of monks they have to support already; and yet others object that those whom they are asked to admit are not sons of their monasteries. Others invoke the strict and blameless life appropriate to religious, saying that these people would be a great nuisance to them, for they are besmirched by many vices and accustomed to live in freedom ... Someone should first ascertain whether recruits   10
to nunneries are inspired to immure themselves for ever out of pure devotion and the desire to be better placed to serve God, or whether they are being forced to become nuns by the fear of their fathers, who have used threats to make them consent to do so with their tongues, but not with their hearts.

The papal nuncio in Venice to Gregory XIII, *c.* 1580

5.9(b)

Since I do not have enough movables, silver and other property at present ... finding that I have so many sons, I ask my daughters to be content to become nuns and to give me this pleasure because I am certain that they will always be happier and believe themselves to be more content when they consider the trials which must be undergone by those who marry.

From the will of Count Francesco Tiepolo, May 1611. Both in *Venice, A Documentary History*, **ed. D. Chambers and B. Pullan, Basil Blackwell Publishers, Oxford, 1992, pp. 206–8, 248–9**

Questions

1 Explain the meaning of 'their mothers' **[5.8 lines 8–9]**.
2 What does **5.8** see as the key problem? What solution is proposed?
3 (a) Why should the author of **5.9(a)** take such an attitude?
   (b) Can we presume to trust his judgement?
4 Explain the conflict of interest between **5.9(a)** and **5.9(b)** over nunneries.

Engagement with the world

Teresa opened her first convent of reformed Carmelites in 1562; de Sales founded the Visitation of St Mary in 1610. Both struggled toward a new definition of the role of nuns appropriate to the challenges of their age. The Visitation was heir to that emphasis within the Catholic Reformation which sought service of God through service to the community: 'Leave God in prayer at the altar. Then find him in the beggar in the gutter' (St Philip Neri, 1594). Innovative and experimental, the Visitation was as revolutionary in concept as the Society of Jesus, shedding externals like special dress, and shows just how deeply the late medieval critique of monasticism had been taken to heart. The Visitation was also an early sign of the enhanced role women were able to take so prominently in 17th-century France. The order served a variety of religious and social needs. First, it met the Tridentine requirement for faith and good works to co-operate in salvation. Second, it addressed the growing social problems of the period by placing social welfare at the heart of its spirituality. Third, its warm ethos gave women called to the religious life the opportunity to enter the hitherto exclusively male domain of silent, contemplative piety and prayer. Fourth, its lack of formal vows offered an organised religious life to the laity, while its gentle lifestyle was consciously designed for those women whose health or temperament would never stand the rigours of the ascetic life practised in traditional reformed nunneries.

As in his hugely popular books of devotions, de Sales offered to ordinary Catholics the possibility of serious piety, stripped bare of its restrictive practices. The holy life was not exclusive, beyond the reach of ordinary people. The holy life was easy. Perfection really was possible, for everyone. Nobody typified better than de Sales the anti-Augustinian direction of post-Tridentine Catholic salvation theology. But his revolutionary departures from orthodox monasticism touched raw nerves. More seriously, it contravened the Tridentine decree of December 1563 requiring the enclosure of nuns. Innovation for female religious was so much harder than for male. Francis de Sales was forced to comply with Tridentine rigour, but he was not prepared to compromise his commitment to 'the contemplative in action'. If the sisters could not go out into the world, they must draw it within their cloister and, taking a concern beloved of Catholic reform, Visitandine nunneries became free boarding schools for poor children.

5.10   Monastic ideals: the gentle vision of St Francis de Sales

This Congregation receives either widows or spinsters, but not children under 17. They do a year of probation or, if necessary, two or three ... After the novitiate, they are solemnly received, but not to vows ... The younger members leave it to serve the poor and the sick ... They wear no habit, but only sober clothing, always with a veil ... They sing only the Office of Our Lady, with a very   5
devotional chant, and have no services during the night hours. In the summer they rise at five and go to bed at ten; in the winter at six and half-past ten. They have an hour's mental prayer in the morning and another hour in the evening. For the rest, they have a discipline of work, silence, obedience, humility and poverty as strict as in any monastery in the world ... They are always to wear   10
shoes and, in winter, a woollen cloak.

Rule of the Visitation of St Mary, July 1610, in *Œuvres de St François*, **XIV, pp. 329–31†**

5.11   Objections to the Visitation Rule

I am unwilling that the Rule as used in Annecy be employed here in Lyons without certain modifications ... The sisters take no formal vows, neither are they enclosed. If they may leave whenever they wish (or whenever their father wishes it), they are not nuns, for where is their obligation? At the first self-doubt or crossed word, they will be off in floods of tears. How can there be stability in   5
such a house? And if there is no stability, what father will permit his daughter to enter such an order? ... The absence of obligation and enclosure for women is

against Trent and is a dangerous innovation, all the more so since it will undermine most holy reform. If this should proceed, the Visitation will become an asylum for nuns running away from their Rule.

Archbishop of Lyons to Francis de Sales, March 1615, in J. F. Gonthier, *Vie de St François de Sales*, Paris, 1917, II, pp. 53–4†

Questions

1 Explain how **5.10** shows the Visitation's commitment to 'activism in grace'.
2 Why were Visitation sisters to wear shoes and a cloak and to have no night services [**5.10**]?
3 (a) 'Convents without rule of enclosure are little better than brothels in Venice' (Pius V, 1571). Assess **5.11**'s concept of the capabilities of nuns.
  (b) What seems to have been the main anxiety of **5.11**?
4 From **5.10** and **5.11**, explain what was innovative about the Visitation and why it fell foul of authority.

Retreat from the world

Unlike de Sales, Teresa positively sought the traditionalist and Tridentine ideal of nuns enclosed within their convent. As neither a bishop nor a man, however, her struggle was far the greater and her trials laid bare many of the assumptions and prejudices of her world. The Carmelite order which she joined in 1535 was not unreformed, but her fellow nuns were outraged by her proposals for faithful observance of their ancient Rule. For a thousand years, retreat from the world had been perceived as the purest form of Christian living. Teresa used that ideal to push at the frontiers of church and society. Her concept of poverty was mendicant. Her nuns would live on donations; they must own no property. She saw such absolute poverty as liberating, for it removed the powerful private interests of noble families who, in exchange for endowments, expected burial for their dead, perpetual prayer for their souls and places for their surplus daughters. At the same time, she attempted an egalitarian admissions policy, in deliberate contrast to the noble rank required of entrants to most Spanish nunneries. Such ideas may also have reflected 'her own sense of alienation from a world of racial and social obsessions' (Weber, 1990). Her family was *converso* (Jews forcibly converted to Christianity) and, therefore, in contemporary Spanish opinion, of no social significance.

Teresa explored the role of Catholic women. With noble patronage removed and the strictest poverty enforced, all recruits would be willing volunteers. Their chastity would also be voluntary and so could be 'a source of pride and independence' (Brown, 1986). Thus far, her thoughts were consistent with reformist nuns across the Christian centuries. Teresa's conversion coincided, however, with the upsurge of militant Calvinism in France and the Netherlands. The medieval church had assigned no specific role to women and the Catholic hierarchy of the 16th and 17th centuries continued to shy away from women having any active religious capability. Unable to be a missionary priest (clearly her heart's desire), her solution was to define a job which, she argued, only women could do properly: nuns would provide 'a praying Counter-Reformation' (Egidio, 1980). Each of the sixteen reformed convents she founded would, through contemplative prayer, strike a direct blow against heresy. But the days of religious innovation ended earlier in Spain than anywhere else. Economic depression, national paranoia and not a little sexual bigotry combined to undermine her ideal. Dependent on communities increasingly hard-pressed by growing poverty, mendicants evoked dwindling sympathy and, as Castile's slump deepened, it destroyed the urban merchant and professional (often *converso*) families who funded them. Teresa compromised and accepted endowments, 'accommodating aristocratic values to ensure survival' (Bilinkoff, 1989). Five years after her death, her order introduced minimum dowry payments of all new nuns. Ten years later, in line with Spain's hysterical obsessions with racial and theological purity, it banned recruits of *converso* descent. Teresa would have been denied admission to her own order.

5.12   Teresa's programme rejected by her own nunnery

[As news of her plans] spread around the place there fell upon us a persecution so severe that it would not be possible to describe it in a few words. They talked, they laughed at us, and they declared that the idea was absurd. Of me they said that I was in the right place where I was, and they subjected my companion to such a persecution that it quite wore her out ... There was so much chatter and   5
fuss in my own convent that the Provincial thought it would be difficult to oppose everybody, and so changed his mind. He now withdrew his backing, saying that the income was not assured, that in any case it would be insufficient, and that the plan was meeting with heavy opposition ... Once it was discontinued and abandoned, people were even more certain that it had all been an absurd   10
feminine whimsy, and gossip at my expense increased ... I was very unpopular throughout the convent for wanting to found a more strictly enclosed house. The nuns said that this was an insult to them; that I could serve God just as well where I was, since there were others there better than myself; that I had no love

for my own house ... I wondered whether I had been guilty of leading others into   15
sin, whether these visions were illusory, whether all my prayer had been a
deception.

The Life of St Teresa of Avila by Herself, written *c*.1557–65, tr. J. M. Cohen,
Penguin Books Ltd, Harmondsworth, 1957, pp. 238, 241–2

5.13   Teresa as radical: poverty and equality

5.13(a)

If, with a good conscience, I could wish that the day you build a costly dwelling
it fell and killed you all, I would beg God for it. It looks very ill, my daughters,
to build fine houses with needy men's alms. God forbid it! ... Everything must
fall at the Day of Judgment. Who knows how soon that may be? It would not
look well if a house of poor women made such a noise when it tumbled; the truly   5
poor make no commotion.

5.13(b)

The thing that clings the closest and is most difficult to shake off is the love of
kindred ... Let the nun who comes from the highest family be the last to mention
her father: we must all be equals here ... O College of Christ which, by His wish,
ranked St Peter the fisherman higher than St Bartholomew.[1] His Majesty foresaw
how the world would wrangle over the question of who was formed in the finest   5
clay – which is like disputing whether clay is fittest for making bricks or a mud
wall. Good God, what a misery this is!

[1] Medieval legend said the Apostle Bartholomew was a Greek prince.

**St Teresa, *The Way of Perfection*, written *c*. 1563–5, tr. F. B. Zimmerman,
London, 1935, pp. 14–15, 159–60**

5.14   Teresa as radical: women as Counter Reformation warriors

I heard of the miseries France was suffering and of the havoc the Lutherans[1]
were making there ... I would have laid down a thousand lives to save one of the
many souls perishing there. Yet, as I am but a woman, feeble and faulty, it was
impossible for me to serve God in the way I wished ... Our defenders need
[God's help] urgently. I wish you to lead such lives as to merit to obtain two   5
favours from God: first that there may be numerous learned theologians to
quench the devouring flames of heresy ... [Second] that when engaged in this
war, our Lord may uphold the priests so that they may escape the many dangers
... Strive so to follow our Rule that our prayers and penances may avail to help

these servants of God ... This is a very special favour, not shared in by the men   10
of whom I have been speaking.

[1] In fact, Huguenots (Calvinists); Philip II's Spain could not tell the difference.

St Teresa, *The Way of Perfection*, pp. 5–6, 17–19, 218

5.15   Teresa blocked: the triumph of noble interests

I in no way wanted to accept [endowment]. The town was so small that we
would be forced to have a fixed income in order to support ourselves: something
to which I was very much opposed ... [My confessor] told me that I was wrong,
that since the holy council had given permission to have an income, I should not,
because of my own opinion, fail to found a monastery where God could be so   5
much served. To this were added the many urgings of the noble lady who wished
to donate the property. How could I refuse?

St Teresa, *The Book of Her Foundations*, written *c*.1573–82, in *The Collected
Works of St Teresa*, tr. K. Kavanaugh and O. Rodriguez, Institute of
Carmelite Studies, Washington, 1985, III, 9:2–3

5.16   Teresa blocked: denial of the feminine

5.16(a)

[She is] a restless gadabout, a disobedient and contumacious woman, who
invented wicked doctrines, called them devotion ... and taught others against
the commands of St Paul, who has forbidden women to teach.

Felipe Sega, papal nuncio, 1579, in *The Complete Works of St Teresa*, tr. E.
Allison Peers, Sheed and Ward, London, 1946, III, p. 150

5.16(b)

This woman ceased to be a woman, restoring herself to the virile[1] state, to greater
glory than if she had been a man from the beginning, for she rectified nature's
error, transforming herself through virtue into the bone[2] from which she sprang.

[1] 'virile': the Spanish word implies the masculine.
[2] 'the bone' = Adam's rib.

Francisco de Jesus, a Carmelite friar, preaching in celebration of
Teresa being made patron saint of Spain, 1627, in A. Weber, *Teresa of
Avila and the Rhetoric of Femininity*, Princeton University Press,
Princeton, 1990, pp. 17–18

Questions

1 (a) List the objections to Teresa's reform raised in **5.12**.
   (b) Which do you think was the most serious? Explain your reasoning.
2 (a) How is strict poverty justified in **5.13(a)**?
   (b) On what basis does Teresa argue for equality in **5.13(b)**?
   (c) Why did she see poverty and equality as inseparable?
   (d) Explain 'The town ... to support ourselves' [**5.15 lines 1–2**].
3 'In the cloister, our nuns will be fighting for Christ' (St Teresa, 1578). With reference to **5.14**, explain what she meant and how she thought the process worked.
4 (a) Of the 63 saints canonised between 1500 and 1700, only nine were women. What do **5.16(a)** and **5.16(b)** suggest was really at stake?
   (b) Does de Sales' experience [**5.11**] confirm that?
   (c) Why might Teresa choose to call herself 'feeble and faulty' [**5.14 line 3**]? Read **8.6(d)** before you answer.

Summary

How far does the evidence in this chapter confirm that 'institutional developments within the Catholic church during the century after Trent show overriding emphasis to assert the values of obedience, hierarchy, deference and conformity, in order to suppress individual and institutional experimentation' (Wright, *The Counter-Reformation*, 1982)?

References

A. Antonovics, 'Counter-Reformation Cardinals, 1534–1590', *European Studies Review*, II, 1972

A. Black, *Monarchy and Community: Political Ideas in the Later Conciliar Controversy*, Cambridge University Press, 1970

J. Brown, *Immodest Acts: The Life of a Lesbian Nun in Renaissance Italy*, Oxford University Press, 1986

T. Egidio, 'The Historical Setting of St Teresa's Life', *Carmelite Studies*, I, 1980

B. Hamilton, *Political Thought in Sixteenth Century Spain*, Clarendon Press, 1963

H. Jedin, *History of the Church: Reformation and Counter Reformation*, Burns and Oates, 1980

A. Weber, *Teresa of Avila and the Rhetoric of Femininity*, Princeton University Press, 1990

For Bilinkoff, Delumeau, Evennett (1968), Prodi and Wright, see *Suggestions for further reading*.

6 Reformation in the parishes: clergy and people

Reform programmes were concerned with more than institutions. Structural renewal was a starting point – and for some senior clergy it was also the finishing point – of the reform agenda. But advancing spiritual revival gradually enabled churchmen to alter their focus and see beyond the organisation to the reason why it existed: to nurture the spiritual and moral health of the people (and the clergy). The Catholic Reformation was in large measure a movement directed by bishops, implemented by parish priests and aimed at the laity. The success of Protestantism displayed the danger inherent in a laity understanding little of their faith. Post-Tridentine priests would have to preach and teach to a degree well beyond anything known before. In the long run, that 'probably had more considerable effects than any other innovation of the 16th century' (Bossy, 1985). Reform was not, however, to be confined to religious instruction. Reformers – Catholic and Protestant alike – sought to transform social and moral attitudes and behaviour. Changes to the law would deliver part of this reformation of manners, as would a deluge of printed literature. But the key instrument of change was to be the parish priest. Yet the clergy were themselves in need of fundamental overhaul. That the confidence (or folly) existed to tackle both, simultaneously, is breath-taking.

The revolution would require a strengthening of the church's position as an institution in society and an increasing ascendancy of the clergy over the daily lives of their parishioners. There would be no drawing together of pastor and people as in Protestant lands, not even a partial one. Rather, the exclusiveness of the priesthood and its unique power to celebrate mass and absolve sin was to be re-emphasised. Every reform step would be dogged by practical difficulty, thick-set inertia and the opposition of entrenched vested interests. Enhanced clerical influence was likely to inflame relations with secular governments, themselves then busily extending their own social jurisdiction over their subjects. An improved clergy suited the secular need for local administrators and, across much of Europe, the priest became an unpaid civil servant. Neither church nor state would argue about the need for greater social control over the people. But when the pre-eminence of the secular state was advancing on all fronts, conflict was guaranteed over whose responsibility it should be. Then, when pressure to change lifestyles began to bite and sin was criminalised, could reform end up being seen as anything other than intrusive and oppressive? Finally, could the deliberate creation of a clerical elite and the establishing of an inquisitorial discipline mean anything but the alienation of the people from their priest? Was reform bound to spawn a new anti-clericalism?

Towards a new parish clergy: an endemic problem

'We have failed to cultivate the field entrusted to us' was the sharp judgement Cardinal Pole presented to his fellow priests at Trent. The reformers' message to the Catholic clergy was as uncompromising as the challenge they set was demanding. The Council left few doubts as to what should be taught and none about whose job it was to teach. The ambiguities and uncertainties which had been so debilitating to early anti-Reformation had been swept away. But that was only the beginning. Until enforced and maintained, Tridentine standards of clerical qualification and commitment were worthless. This section takes France as a case study because that forces us to realise the extended timescale over which the Catholic Reformation took root and then bore its remarkable fruit. While Italy and Spain stepped briskly off the mark, French spiritual renewal lagged well behind, mirroring deep political and economic sickness. Unlike the briefly restored Catholic hierarchy in England under Cardinal Pole, the French church did not begin to reform itself during Trent. Once the Council ended, the Wars of Religion had already started and that made reform very much harder. Whether the bishops even wanted to try is doubtful. Only the succession crisis of 1589–93 when the monarchy became Protestant 'jolted the church out of its inertia' (Benedict, 1981) and strong sense of self-sufficiency. But it emerged from the wars in chronic disorder. Absenteeism was rife. One-third of bishoprics were vacant and barely 10 per cent enjoyed a resident prelate. Churches were badly damaged or in ruins – in some dioceses up to 80 per cent. Order returned slowly. The Estates-General permitted the publication of Trent's decrees only in 1614, which in turn meant that France's bishops did not declare their intention to implement Tridentine-style reform until July 1615. Heroic inspiration for a new-model priest and pastor, animated by the Renaissance urge to action and driven by an ideal of devoted, selfless service, was provided by the Bishop of Geneva, St Francis de Sales (d. 1622) and the Parisian cleric St Vincent de Paul (d. 1660). The result was 'a phenomenal development in spirituality' (Evennett, 1968), but it took two generations to accomplish the structural changes and a third to blossom. In the Empire and Hungary, full-blown Tridentine reform was similarly delayed until the later 17th and early 18th centuries.

Even then, how comprehensive and how effective reform had been is open to question. Despite Tridentine prohibitions, abuses like pluralism were phased out, rather than swept away. In 1615, one-quarter of the 108 French bishops were not ordained priests, one-third were regular absentees and two-thirds never held a diocesan synod. Upon such men waited the initial and thus perhaps the most vital stages of reform. The question of seminary training illustrates precisely the reality of French reform. Seminaries were intended by Trent to revolutionise the clergy. Yet only a handful had opened north of the Alps or Pyrenees before 1650, attendance was never compulsory for ordinands and many were 'no more than glorified grammar schools' (Bergin, 1992). Although most taught a limited theological curriculum, their graduates were most certainly better educated (intellectually and morally) than medieval priests. But were they any better trained in being priests? None of the seminaries scratched the surface of pastoral questions even though, especially for those working in rural France, nothing would have been more useful than training in how to deal with the crises of life and death their parishioners would bring them. Nor was any attempt made to redraw unmanageably large rural parish boundaries. From diocese to diocese, standards varied quite considerably. We already know that, in matters of reform, there was neither unity of method nor of purpose across the Catholic world. But the degree of variation remains to be established, as does the extent to which reform penetrated. While we know that the minimum at least was performed, 'we cannot be certain in what spirit or with what degree of insight it was done' (Green, 1989).

6.1 Clerical inadequacies

6.1(a)

The church faces ruin in many places because of the bad lives led by priests. Their calling is to lead the people into piety, but how can this be when so many are without piety themselves, ignorant of the sacred scriptures, absent from their cures or lost in sins of the flesh? A priest wrote to me saying, 'In this diocese the clergy know no discipline, the people know no fear, the priests know no charity.   5 The pulpits have no preachers, learning is not honoured, vice is not chastised and the church's authority is either hated or despised.' Lord Jesu, what is to be done?

Vincent de Paul, 1644, in L. Abelly, *La Vie du vénérable serviteur de Dieu*, Paris, 1664, II, p. 213†

6.1(b)

Ah, if you only saw the ugly and different ways mass was celebrated 40 years ago, you would have felt ashamed. There was nothing more ugly in the world ... Some started off with the *Our Father*; others, taking their vestments in hand, would start to say the service before they were properly dressed. Once when at St Germain I noticed seven or eight priests all saying mass differently. There was   5 such a diversity that you would have wept to see it.

Vincent de Paul addressing a diocesan synod, 1659, in *St Vincent de Paul: Correspondance*, ed. P. Coste, Paris, 1920, XII, p. 258†

6.2   A new clerical image

Nothing instructs the faithful to true piety and reverence for the Almighty more than the daily life and example of those called and dedicated to the sacred priesthood. As they are seen to have been raised to a sublime estate above the things of this world, so all eyes will be trained upon them as upon a mirror and take from them a pattern to be imitated. It is not long since that most priests   5 here were indistinguishable from the peasantry. They looked like peasants, they behaved like peasants and thus they received neither love nor respect ...

Live therefore each hour as if the salvation of a soul depended upon it. Watch yourself. Remember that you are set apart from the common as a father from his children. Be neither quarrelsome nor troublesome. Abstain from bad company,   10 from those notorious as drunkards or gamblers ... A priest should never hunt. In public, be meticulous to dress as befits your state, in sober black and with a hat, avoiding unseemly ornament whether coloured stockings and gloves or a wig ... Under no circumstances must you ever engage in trade or perform manual labour in the fields.

From a sermon to ordinands, *c.*1665, in Abbé de Beaumont, *Histoire du diocèse de Nîmes jusqu'à 1789*, Montpellier, 1910, p. 149†

6.3   In-service training

6.3(a)   Parish missions

Where the priest is ignorant,[1] lend him your books, recommending passages for study and discussing them with him. Whatever his condition, seize the opportunity to educate him as well as his people. He is a fellow preacher of Jesus.

His business is the salvation of souls, so help him to perform that sacred task to greater effect ... Make sure that he never allows fairs and other celebrations to   5
take place on Sundays or holy days, that the taverns are kept shut during service and that the church is never used as a market (or for other profane use).

¹ The diocesan seminary was founded in 1650.

Instructions for a Jesuit mission, diocese of Coutances, 1674, in G. Bonnenfant, *Les Seminaires normandes du XVI au XVIII siècles*, Paris, 1915, p. 117†

6.3(b) Cathedral lecturers

That the clergy may not suffer, there are now masters of grammar and of theology attached to the cathedral,¹ drawn from the friars and selected by myself with the object of maintaining a knowledge of Latin and of theology. In particular, they are to advise on cases of conscience for the benefit of confessors and all with cure of souls.

¹ Cathedral lecturers were first ordered by the IVth Lateran Council, 1215.

From a report of the Bishop of Troyes to Louis XIV, 1687, in A. Prévost, *Le Diocèse de Troyes*, Troyes, 1908, p. 174†

6.3(c) Diocesan synods

In obedience to the decree of the Holy Council [of Trent], long ignored to the hurt of this diocese and the church, it is my intention to establish a synod of all the clergy under my spiritual care ... Look upon it as a means whereby you may better serve Our Lord for it will enable you the better to discharge your duty to God and to your parishioners. The business of the synod shall be a lecture of   5
instruction on a point of doctrine and another on a question relating to the direction of souls. Priests among you who hold the degree in sacred theology shall be appointed to deliver the lectures and, after each synod, it shall be their duty also to send to the bishops a written report, noting in particular the opinions of young priests ... By this means, think also that you shall be   10
strengthening the bond between yourself and your brother priests. The synod shall be to you as a sacred society.

Orders for the synod, diocese of Gap, 1686, in E. Jacques, *Le Seminaire de Gap, 1577–1789*, Gap, 1924, p. 61†

6.4   The very model of a Tridentine priest

6.4(a)

The duty of following in the footsteps of Christ is most strictly binding on the
priesthood. They are bound to follow not from afar but closely ... Never permit
any excuse to turn you from preaching. Preach simply, on useful subjects. Do not
waste time constructing elaborate sermons fit for publication. Preach rather as a
father, from the heart, without artificial style or gesture.   5
[1634]

6.4(b)

One Sunday as I was robing for the Holy Mass, word was brought that in an
isolated house a quarter of a league away, everyone was ill and all were in great
need. I had only to mention this in my sermon when God touched the hearts of
those who heard me and they found themselves deeply moved with compassion ...
I suggested to my dear people that they should take turns to visit them and cook   5
for them, not only for the family in question, but for similar cases that might
arise, aiding them corporally with good food and medicines, and spiritually by
disposing the dying to die well and those who would recover to live a better life
... As servants of the poor, we must tend those in need as we would our own,
indeed as we would care for Our Lord himself who counts as done to Himself   10
what we do for the poor.
[1617]

6.4(c)

In the confessional, aim to convert to penitence rather than to make them afraid.
Remember, your task is to encourage in the people not hatred but the love of
God. Leave everything when the call comes. Never turn anyone away. Neither
hurry them, but gently lead them, stumbling and embarrassed before the throne
of the Almighty with words such as 'God is waiting for you to open your heart.   5
Can't you see him? He is there, holding out his arms to you.' And afterwards,
give words of encouragement, like 'How dear your soul is to me' and 'There is
joy in heaven now.'
[1625]

**All extracts from Coste, *Vincent de Paul: Correspondance*, XIII, pp. 423–5,
XII, pp. 193, 211†**

Questions

1   Explain the meaning in **6.3(b)** of:
    (i)   'cases of conscience' [**line 4**]
    (ii) 'cure of souls' [**line 5**].
2   (a) What does **6.1(a)** see as being wrong with the French clergy?
    (b) How did those faults breach **4.10**?
3   (a) What does **6.1(b)** tell us about the reformist agenda?
    (b) From **6.2**, explain how reformers wanted to change the image of
         the clergy.
    (c) What is meant by the last two sentences of **6.3(c)**?
    (d) Explain the significance of the final sentence in **6.3(a)**.
4   Assess the relative values of the training methods in **6.3(a)–(c)**.
5   Can we deduce from **6.3(a)–(c)** that **4.11** was a worthless decree?
    Explain your answer.
6   How does Vincent de Paul seek in **6.4(a)–(c)** to remedy the faults he
    complains of in **6.1(a) and (b)**?
7   Using **6.1–6.4** and **4.10–4.12**, write a job description for a Catholic
    Reformation model priest.

Art in the service of religion

This section does not examine the dramatic upsurge in new religious building and decoration commissioned by or for the Catholic church in the two
centuries after Trent. Rather it sketches briefly the framework in which
those works were produced. The needs of reform revolutionised the design
of churches. Sermons became so significant that, across Catholic
Christendom, the body of the building was turned into a wide and well-lit
auditorium. To the edge of that space was brought the altar and the celebration of mass. Congregations could now hear, could now see and could
thus now participate. Yet for all the new emphasis on intellectual understanding, reformed Catholicism never devalued its profound appreciation of
the ability of sacred images 'to engulf all the senses of those who experienced
it' (Scarisbrick, 1988). Religious art was an incitement to piety, a means of
salvation, a most persuasive instrument of education and propaganda.
Paintings and statues must be ideologically sound. Nothing must mislead the
faithful. Nothing must give the heretics grounds for ridiculing the faith.
While there was never any attempt to impose one style, and the virtues
of sumptuous decoration were hotly debated, churchmen were agreed that

the clarity of the message was the primary concern. Artists had become preachers.

6.5   Architecture and acoustics

I recommend that all the chapels and the choir be vaulted, because the word or song of the priest echoes better from the vault than it would from rafters. But in the nave of the church, where there will be sermons, I recommend a flat wooden ceiling so the voice of the preacher may not escape, nor re-echo from the vaults.

Francesco Giorgi on the building of S. Francesco della Vigna, Venice, 1535, in R. Wittkower, *Architectural Principles in the Age of Humanism*, Warburg Institute, London, 1949, p. 15

6.6   Regulations for church art

No image shall be set up which is suggestive of false doctrine or which may furnish an occasion of dangerous error to the uneducated ... No one [shall] be allowed to place or cause to be placed any unusual image in any church ... unless it be approved by the bishop ... All lasciviousness must be avoided so that figures shall not be painted or adorned with a beauty inciting to lust.

Decree of the Council of Trent, December 1563, in Schroeder, *Canons and Decrees*, pp. 216–17

6.7   Art and artist in the service of the faith

Since Our Lord God desires everyone to praise Him with his body and soul, holy images help to express outwardly the reverence that we have within us, and allow us to dedicate this reverence to God as an oblation and kind of sacrifice ... It would be hard to overstate the good that holy images do: they perfect our understanding, move our will, refresh our memory of divine things. They   5
heighten our spirits ... and show to our eyes and hearts the heroic and magnanimous acts of patience, of justice, chastity, meekness, charity and contempt for worldly things in such a way that they instantly cause us to seek virtue and to shun vice, and thus put us on the roads that lead to blessedness.

   Besides what has been said, there is another very important aspect of Christian   10
painting, which concerns the goal of the Catholic painter, who, in the guise of a preacher, endeavours to persuade the people and to bring them, by means of his painting, to embrace religion ... As the means of the orator is speaking appropriately and to the point, so his end will be to convince us ... Thus the painter, like the orator, will be obliged to paint in such a way that he attains the   15
desired end by means of sacred images. Would that our painters nowadays

realized these obligations; but how many of them are capable of understanding these words of mine? Oh, what a shame it is, what a terrible shame!

Pacheco was himself both a painter and inspector of art for the Inquisition in the diocese of Seville.

Francisco Pacheco, *The Art of the Painter*, Seville, 1649, in R. Enggass and J. Brown, *Italy and Spain, 1600–1700, Sources and Documents in the History of Art*, Prentice-Hall, Englewood Cliffs, 1970, pp. 163–4

6.8   A picture under scrutiny

Said to him, 'Have you painted any Suppers[1] other than this one?'
    He answered, 'Yes, my lords.'
    Said to him, 'How many have you painted, and in what places?' ...
    Said to him, 'What is the meaning of those armed men, dressed in the German style, each with a halberd in his hand?'   5
    He answered, 'I must say a few words here.'
    He was told to say them.
    He answered, 'We painters take the same licence as do poets and madmen, and so I made those two halberdiers, one of them drinking and the other eating ... to be ready to perform some task, for I thought it fitting that the owner of the   10
house (who, as I have been told, was a great and rich man) should have such servants.'
    Said to him, 'And that man dressed as a clown, with a parrot on his fist, for what purpose did you paint him on the canvas?'
    He answered, 'For ornament, as one does.'   15
    Said to him, 'Who are at the Lord's table?'
    He answered, 'The twelve apostles.'
    Said to him, 'What is St Peter, the first of them, doing?'
    He answered, 'Dividing the lamb, to give it to the other head of the table' ...
    Said to him, 'Explain what the next one is doing.'   20
    He answered, 'There is a man who has a fork and is attending to his teeth.'
    Said to him, 'Who do you think was really present at that supper?'
    He answered, 'I believe that Christ and his apostles were present. But if there is space left over ... I decorate it with figures of my own invention.'
    Said to him, 'Did anyone commission you to paint Germans and clowns and   25
the like in that picture?'
    He answered, 'No, my lords; my commission was to adorn that picture as I saw fit, for it is large and can include many figures ...'
    He was asked, 'Did he think it proper to depict at the Lord's last supper clowns, drunkards, Germans, dwarfs and other lewd things?'   30
    He answered, 'No, my lords.'
    He was asked, 'Why, then, did you paint them?'

He answered, 'I did them on the understanding that they are not within the place where the supper is being held.'

He was asked, 'Do you not know that in Germany and other places infected with heresy they are accustomed, by means of outlandish paintings full of indecencies and other devices, to abuse, mock and pour scorn on things of the Holy Catholic Church, in order to teach false doctrine to foolish and ignorant people?' 35

He answered, 'I agree, my lord, that it is bad.' 40

Said to him, 'Do you think that you did well to paint this picture ... and do you wish to maintain that it is seemly?'

He answered, 'Most noble lord, I do not wish to defend it. But I did think I was doing right. I did not think of such important things.'

After which their lordships determined that the said Master Paolo should be compelled to correct and amend the picture considered at this session, as the Holy Office sees fit, within the space of three months, this correction to be carried out at the discretion of the Holy Office, at his expense, and under threat of penalties to be imposed by the Holy Office. 45

¹ Ordered as *The Last Supper* for a monastic refectory, it now hangs in the Accademia (Venice) as *Feast in the House of Levi.*

From the trial of Paolo Veronese by the Inquisition, Venice, July 1573, in Chambers and Pullan, *Venice*, pp. 233–6

Questions

1   (a)   What were 'the chapels and the choir' used for [**6.5 line 1**]?
    (b)   Search the illustrations in books on architectural history for examples of church design 1500–1750. Do they suggest reform ideas were effective?

2   'Pagan images shock the saints in heaven' (Possevino, *Treatise on Poetry and Painting*, 1595). How does **6.7** reveal the concerns behind **6.6**?

3   (a)   Explain the purpose of the first two questions in **6.8**.
    (b)   Why should German soldiers arouse Inquisitorial interest [**6.8 lines 4–5**]?
    (c)   On what other grounds did the Inquisition object to this painting?
    (d)   Do they show that Tridentine regulations had been extended? Explain.
    (e)   Consider whether **6.7** would have backed Veronese or his accusers.
    (f)   Veronese appeased the Inquisition simply by changing the painting's title. Comment.

Charity

'Love ought to manifest itself in deeds, not words' wrote St Thomas of Villanueva, Archbishop of Valencia (d. 1555). Trent's firm endorsement of the idea that active co-operation in God's work was essential to individual salvation gave dynamic strength to the Catholic Reformation's commitment to seek Christ among the poor. Reformed Catholicism, just as much as Protestantism, was overwhelmingly concerned with the relationship of each individual to God and the doing of the divine will, a double discipline deriving primarily from 15th-century Italian confraternities and oratories. The outcome was an active spirituality, a charitable imperative, unlike anything Christianity had yet experienced: 'Action was prayer and prayer led to action' (Evennett, 1968). The Protestants had misjudged human capabilities. Individuals could tell right from wrong and themselves choose to do right. Guided by their priest in the regular privacy of confession, self-discipline, good works and social responsibility could all be fostered. At one level, to live a life guided by such principles was an act of counter reformation for it was a daily denial of justification by faith alone. At another, Catholic Reformation activism in grace was engaged in combat with the self, with the impulses to good or evil. Morality as well as theology was at issue. So too was the relationship between clergy and laity. Almost everywhere, the call to virtue marked 'the final triumph of medieval intervention by ecclesiastical authority in the affairs of lay charities and religious confraternities' (Pullan, 1971). These societies with their chapels, their banners, their processions and their rituals dedicated to the Virgin Mary, the Sacred Heart, the Blessed Sacrament or the Rosary flourished as never before. Direction of their programmes of social work and control over their devotions fell to the clergy even before Clement VIII placed them all under episcopal control in 1604.

Not so the burgeoning problem of poor relief: 'No era had ever been so conscious of the poor' (Kamen, 1976). At least one-fifth of a town's population in 1600 would have been beggars and vagabonds. Faced by swollen ranks of vagrant paupers, magistrates turned away from traditional reliance on private, voluntary (and thus, as they saw it, haphazard and inefficient) donations to more structured programmes. Widespread begging had become more than an embarrassment; it was now seen as a threat to social stability, even as a crime. The friars stoutly resisted this development, upholding the medieval notion that the poor deserved sympathy and assistance, that begging was honourable in itself and necessary if Christians (i.e. potential donors) were to be confronted with moral choice and enabled to perform spiritually beneficial acts of charity. But unprecedented numbers of vagrants guaranteed that heightened social tension eroded traditional sympathies. In economies that created permanent underemployment, 'outdoor relief' seemed only to encourage antisocial idleness, criminality and rebellion. The poor had become a burden, poverty a social disorder. Some confraternities ended open charity and restricted the giving of food, blankets, shelter or medicine to those able to recite the Lord's Prayer or catechism. Across Christendom (Protestant as well as Catholic), begging was restricted or banned, vagrants were driven off or sent to the galleys and the remainder forcibly removed from the streets into institutions. In the vacuum created by this 'decline in the spirit of neighbourliness' (Galpern, 1976), poor relief passed into secular hands. Clerical influence might ameliorate the punitive, repressive system, but priest and magistrate were moving in the same direction.

6.9   The motives of charity

6.9(a)

It is not enough to proffer aid to the needy: it is vital that this transaction ... should proceed from the true sentiment of the love of God, for, if we bestirred ourselves to help our neighbour from any other motive, the service we did him would be unacceptable to God ... We have need to serve, to become collaborators of Jesus Christ in procuring the salvation of souls.

Sermon at the opening of a refuge for child prostitutes, 1588

6.9(b)

[Those receiving charity are to be told] to give thanks to God, to pray for their benefactors (and especially for the Venetian state), to bear their misfortunes with patience, to take care that their children go and learn Christian doctrine and their girls do not stray into error, to live as good Christians, to engage in frequent devotions, and to apply themselves to some virtuous employment.

Orders of a society distributing food and blankets, 1595

6.9(c)

[How long must we suffer] the immense gravity of the sins committed by night in public streets and other public places by beggars; the poverty of many others, which eventually brings them to die on the streets like dumb brutes in the sight of everyone and without the sacraments of Holy Church; and their misbehaviour,

especially in churches, which disturbs the prayers of the devout to the grave   5
scandal of everyone.

**Proposal to turn a leper hospital into one for beggars, 1594. All extracts
from B. Pullan, *Rich and Poor in Renaissance Venice*, Basil Blackwell
Publishers, Oxford, 1971, pp. 402–3, 387, 374**

6.10   What to do with beggars?

6.10(a)

No man of sense should doubt it is better to cure the afflicted man than to give
him every day a penny ... We do not read that Christ extended to beggars any
charity other than to take away from them the occasion to beg: giving them
health so they could earn without the shame of begging ... Although many
occasions for acquiring personal merit are removed if there are hospitals endowed   5
with revenues, the man who builds these institutions is doing the greatest good.

**Juan de Medina, a Benedictine abbot, *Plan for Poor Relief*, Toledo, 1545,
in Pullan, *Renaissance Venice*, pp. 284–5**

6.10(b)

This is a question of mercy, not of justice. Mercy is an act of pure grace,
performed willingly in imitation of Christ and rendered to one who in no way
deserves help ... No Christian must be denied the opportunity to perform acts of
mercy. Yet when city authorities sweep up their beggars, removing them to the
shadows, they deprive thereby the pauper of his right to beg and the citizen of   5
opportunity to be merciful ... And when those liberties are removed, what is the
result? The pauper becomes an obligation, a burden on the civic purse.

**Domingo Soto, a Dominican theologian, *Considerations of the Poor*,
Salamanca, 1545, ff. 21, 26–7, 30†**

6.10(c)

Religion and justice demand the assistance of the poor. Of the duties of a
Christian monarch, none is greater, none more sublime ... While the citizen is
bound to assist the poor, the obligation of the State is the greater. Indeed, where
private charity is lacking or cannot meet need, it is the public duty of the State to
compel citizens to charity by collecting taxes for poor relief.

**Juan de Mariana, a Jesuit theologian, *Of Royal Institutions*, Madrid, 1599,
ff. 95–6†**

Questions

1   Classify the motives for charity in **6.9** according to the following priorities: material welfare, the salvation of souls, public order.
2   Explain the meaning of 'many occasions for acquiring personal merit' [**6.10(a) lines 4–5**].
3   Put in your own words the issues which divided the authors of **6.10(a)–(c)**.
4   Explain why **6.10(b)** found no favour with secular authorities.
5   'That the soul is without inherent justice is a most pestiferous doctrine' (Cardinal Bellarmine, 1596). Explain how Catholic Reformation views on charity reflect Reformation controversies on salvation.

Morality

Nothing symbolises better the battle with the self, the drive to alter behaviour and the call to virtue than Catholic Reformation penitential saints: saints at their moment of conversion, saints contemplating human mortality, saints practising self-denial. Of these, none was as widely used as Mary Magdalen, the reformed prostitute whose biblical story was used to represent shame over sin and the redemptive power of penance. As devotion to her cult was encouraged, the church broadcast the idea that, in a wicked world, nobody was beyond salvation. Convinced that standards of morality stood at an all-time low, Savonarola had pointed Florence in the 1490s towards communal as well as individual purification. Bishops in the 16th century pursued the quest and, gradually, its zealous hope spread. In the crusade for new codes of personal morality and social discipline, the corrupting influences of everything from cosmetics to theatres and alehouses were deplored.

One area the clergy tried hard to direct were the relationships between husbands and wives, parents and children, masters and servants. While an official view was rarely developed on any question, traditional assumptions were frequently altered. To the well-established medieval notion of a mother's duty to her children was added a wholly new emphasis on the duty of a wife to her husband. Divinely appointed authority, whether of husbands, fathers or masters, was reinforced and probably increased 'in line with the revival of Roman law and the needs of absolute monarchy' (Mousnier, 1974). But arbitrary authority was moderated by new concepts of two-way responsibility. The role of fathers in bringing up their children received a stress quite unknown to medieval men. Love, affection and attachment began to be encouraged as virtues in a father. In the government of the household, Catholic Reformation moralists 'denounced the excesses of marital and paternal power, with a view to attaching men more firmly to their families and inculcating in them the idea that fatherhood meant service, not power' (Flandrin, 1979). The change of expectation is shown vividly in the rehabilitation of St Joseph. A doddering, reluctant husband made fun of or ignored completely in medieval nativity stories and pictures, his feast was approved for local use in 1479 and so powerfully did the cult develop that the feast became obligatory in 1621. Joseph was now depicted as young and vigorous. His fatherly care for the young Jesus and his love for Mary were emphasised, notably by St Teresa of Avila and St Francis de Sales. In the cult of the Holy Family, domestic morality was being refashioned.

Sexual behaviour within the family was another prime target. One question tackled was the 'conjugal debt', the idea that a wife must submit to her husband's sexual demands. This question touched several raw nerves for, if it were even to be qualified, women would be permitted to control their own sexuality and to practise birth control. To a man, medieval theologians had taken both as signs of decadent morals. But Catholic Reformation confessors began to take seriously the needs of their female penitents, their anxiety about endless pregnancies and the very real danger each posed. Meanwhile, the moral theologians launched a sustained attack on age-old sleeping arrangements in which entire families, their servants and any visitors slept in the same room, very possibly in the same bed. Only very slowly, however, was this near-universal rural custom suppressed, its stubborn survival due partly to the extremely high cost of beds and, given the scarcity of fuel, the need for warmth which in turn created in peasant society 'one of the bases of the cohesion of the family' (Flandrin, 1979). Priest and people no longer shared the same values.

6.11   Reformation of manners

6.11(a)

The Fathers[1] were models of virtue to the gentry, something badly needed in those parts ... Drunkenness, swearing and adultery have been beaten back. The face of this city has been changed. Our cathedral was full each time they preached, gave instruction or heard confession ... I myself owe the salvation of my soul to them.

[1] Oratorians conducting an Irish mission, 1646–8.

Edmund O'Dwyer, Bishop of Limerick, to Vincent de Paul, 1648, in Coste, *Vincent de Paul: Correspondance*, IV, p. 340†

6.11(b)

You shall denounce from the altar that near-general habit of families putting
into a common bed sisters and brothers above the age of nine to sleep with
their parents, other relatives or servants. This is a most dreadful vice, an
encouragement to evil, whether through shameful thoughts or the loss of chastity
for it is an assault on purity. Apply yourself to make your parishioners see the   5
great sin they commit.

From 'Injunctions to the Clergy of Troyes', 1636, in C. Lalore, *Ancienne
Discipline du diocèse du Troyes*, **Troyes, 1882, II, p. 41†**

6.11(c)

Why do you rush to dress in clothes of the latest fashion? Why do you spend
long hours before the mirror covering your face with powders? What you clothe
and paint is soon to be devoured by worms. As our years are short, do not waste
yourself and your husband's money on things so transient. You encourage only
pride in yourself, and jealousy and lust among others.

Michel Goffard, a Jesuit, *L'Instruction pour les épouses*, **Lyons, 1616, p. 32†**

6.12   Manuals for the confessional on household government

6.12(a)

The wife who does not wish to obey her husband in matters touching the
government of the family and of the house, and those concerning virtues and
good morals, sins. For the wife is obliged to carry out the commandments of her
husband. If, on the contrary, she tries to assume the government of the house,
pertinaciously and against the will of her husband when he forbids it for some   5
good reason, she sins, for she must do nothing against her husband, to whom she
is subject by divine and human law.

6.12(b)

He who severely and atrociously beats or chastises his wife, even if it be for some
fault, sins. He must chastise her gently and not with cruelty ... [and] the wife
commits no sin if she separates from her husband on account of his cruelty ...
[He may] not overstep the bounds of modesty and reason. For, even though she
is inferior, nevertheless she is not the slave or chambermaid, but the companion   5
and flesh and blood of her husband.

Both extracts from Jean Benedicti, *La Somme des péchez*, **1601**

6.12(c)

[The fourth] commandment imposes obligations not only on children towards their fathers, but also on fathers and mothers towards their children, inasmuch as love should be reciprocal ... God, when he commands children to love and honour their fathers, tacitly enjoins fathers to love their children, and there is no need for Him to do so explicitly, seeing that love of fathers for their children is   5
so natural.

Cardinal Richelieu, *Instruction du Chrestien*, 1640. All extracts from J. L. Flandrin, *Families in Former Times: Kinship, Household and Sexuality*, Cambridge University Press, 1979, pp. 126, 128–9, 138

6.13   St Joseph as seen by St Teresa

I took as my lord and advocate the glorious St Joseph, commending myself earnestly to him ... I am amazed at the great mercies which the Lord has done me through this blessed saint, and from what perils, both of body and soul, he has delivered me. The Lord seems to have given other saints grace to help in some troubles, but I know by experience that this glorious saint helps in all. For   5
His Majesty wishes to teach us that, as He was Himself subject to him on earth – for having the title of father, though only his guardian, St Joseph could command him – so in heaven the Lord does what he asks ... I have never known anyone who was truly devoted to him and offered him particular service who did not visibly increase in virtue, for he gives very real help to those souls who commend   10
themselves to him. For some years now I have always made some request of him on each of his festival days, and it has always been granted. If my petition is wrong in any way, he corrects it for my greater good ... Persons who practise prayer, in particular, should always be his devotees. I do not know how anyone can think of the Queen of the Angels, during the time when she suffered so   15
much with the infant Jesus, without giving thanks to St Joseph for the help he then gave them. If anyone cannot find a master to teach him prayer, he should take this glorious saint for master, and he will not go astray on the road.

Cohen, *Teresa of Avila*, pp. 47–8

6.14 'The saints are as mirrors' (Pius V, 1571)

Joseph's downcast eyes express tenderness and devotion. He holds a shepherd's crook and is crowned by angels for his work. Jesus' outward look engages the viewer and invites contemplation of the saint. This was the main altarpiece of the first western church ever dedicated to this saint, the Chapel of St Joseph, Toledo, built in 1564.

El Greco, *St Joseph and the Christ Child*, Spanish, *c.* 1597–9 (Museo de Santa Cruz, Toledo)

6.15 A model for repentance

The prostitute Mary sits alone. She could be preparing for her next customer, but her jewellery lies abandoned and she looks into a mirror, symbol of differing realities, of vanity and truth. This is the moment of conversion. The domestic setting encourages the viewer to understand and copy Mary's experience, while the lack of background concentrates the eye onto the saint's revelation.

Georges de la Tour, *The Penitent Magdalen*, French, *c.* 1635 (Metropolitan Museum of Art, New York)

6.16   Sexual obligation within marriage?

6.16(a)

A wife may not refuse her husband, but must always submit to his embrace for otherwise she sins. She is under obligation. Were this not so, he might fall into temptation.

Jean Tabourot, *Instruction pour les curés sur toutes les commandements*, Paris, 1591, p. 40†

6.16(b)

[A nursing mother] is dispensed from the obligation of rendering the due, ... [for she] knows from experience that her breasts dry up when she conceives or that her milk becomes very injurious to the child ...
I shall not condemn the man who demands [the conjugal due], because it is justified to imperil one's child so as not to be forced to practise continence for   5
such a long time, which is so very difficult, or rather morally impossible.

Thomas Sanchez, *Disputationem de sancto matrimonii sacramento*, Antwerp, 1607

6.16(c)

In good conscience, [she cannot] render this due when that ... would greatly prejudice health, or life might depend on it ... To this God has never intended to obligate women ... for that would truly be an oppression, and the most severe and intolerable obedience and law ever to be seen among Christians ... This is, therefore, far removed from the fantasy or frenzy of those sensual men who   5
desire that, without exception or demur, their wives should be obliged to acquiesce in and submit to their passions. No, this is an error, an act of impiety and a tyrannical abuse, that destroys such a society and sacrament of love and reciprocal charity.

Pierre Milhard, *Inventaire des cas de conscience*, Paris, 1611. Extracts (b) and (c) from Flandrin, *Families in Former Times*, pp. 237, 207, 218

Questions

1   How would you characterise the view of the ideal household in **6.12**?
2   (a)   How does St Teresa argue for devotion to St Joseph [**6.13**]?
      (b)   Consider how that might reflect the needs of a new cult.
3   'The saint is crowned for his good works. The theme is redemption,
      the doctrine Tridentine' (Davies, 'El Greco and the Spiritual Reform
      Movements in Spain', 1984). Comment on the ways **6.14** promotes
      responsible fatherhood.
4   Look at **6.15** as an object of religious contemplation:
      (i)   Why should the mirror face directly out to the viewer?
      (ii)   Explain why the Magdalen was a perfect model for repentance.
5   (a)   Is **6.16(b)** concerned with the woman, the child or the man?
      (b)   What image of men emerges from **6.16(a)–(c)**?
6   What do **6.11–6.16** tell us about clerical campaigns to reform morals?

Summary

  (i)   'Work as if everything depended on you. Pray as if everything
           depended on God' (St Ignatius Loyola, 1552).
 (ii)   'The first object was not to reform the church, but to re-order lives to
           the doing of God's will and the bringing of benefit to one's neighbour'
           (Evennett, 'The Counter-Reformation', 1965).
(iii)   'The expectation that the majority of people were capable of radical
           religious enlightenment and moral transformation, whether by
           persuasion or coercion, was naive in the extreme' (Ozment, *The Age of
           Reform*, 1980).
(iv)   'Reform weighed heavily on the private individual. At home as at
           work, attitudes and behaviour were to be remodelled. Nothing seemed
           beyond the interest of someone in authority' (Foucault, *Madness and
           Civilization*, 1967).
How well do these statements sum up the new regime brought by Catholic
reform?

References

P. Benedict, *Rouen during the Wars of Religion*, Cambridge University Press, 1981
J. Bergin, 'Between Estate and Profession: The Catholic Parish Clergy of Early
      Modern Western Europe', in *Social Orders and Social Classes in Europe since
      1500*, ed. M. Bush, Longman, 1992

D. Davies, 'El Greco and the Spiritual Reform Movements in Spain', *Studies in the History of Art*, XIII, 1984

H. Evennett, 'The Counter-Reformation', in *The Reformation Crisis*, ed. J. Hurstfield, Edward Arnold, 1965

J. Flandrin, *Families in Former Times: Kinship, Household and Sexuality*, Cambridge University Press, 1979

M. Foucault, *Madness and Civilization: A History of Insanity in the Age of Reason*, Tavistock, 1967

A. Galpern, *The Religions of the People in Sixteenth-Century Champagne*, Harvard University Press, 1976

I. Green, 'Reformed Pastors and *Bons Curés*: The Changing Role of the Parish Clergy in Early Modern Europe', *Studies in Church History*, XXVI, 1989

H. Kamen, *The Iron Century: Social Change in Europe, 1550–1660*, Cardinal, 1976

R. Mousnier, *Les Institutions de la France sous la monarchie absolue*, PUF, Paris, 1974

S. Ozment, *The Age of Reform, 1250–1550*, Yale University Press, 1980

For Bossy (1985), Evennett (1968), Pullan and Scarisbrick, see *Suggestions for further reading*.

7 The impact of reform: three problems

1 The problem of popular religion

New-model clergy, taking the faith to the people, were shocked by the widespread ignorance they found. The faithful, it seemed, knew little and understood even less of what it meant to be a Catholic. We cannot explain that merely by indicting the medieval church. Few in 1400 expected the people to know or to understand, so they were not taught. But reform altered expectations. That was why the question of 'popular religion' caused such a stir. Zealous reformers were outraged to discover, as Christian reformers have always discovered, that although religion as prescribed by the church was accepted and observed, it had limited boundaries. Beyond those boundaries lay 'an extensive religion as practiced by the people which, from the clerical heights, seemed nothing less than deformed, superstitious, even idolatrous' (Christian, 1981).

'Popular religion', as historians uncomfortably term it, has not proved easy to understand. Few agree on what it means or whether it is even valid to attempt to distinguish between 'religion' and 'superstition'. Several fundamentals are, however, clear. Beliefs and practices were uniform neither across Christendom nor from age to age. Those beliefs and practices must not be dismissed with disdain as the folk rituals of ignorant peasants. It is highly artificial to talk of 'popular' and 'elite' cultures. From the late 16th century it may have been fashionable to ridicule the foolishness of common belief. But this was the great age of alchemy and astrology. Kings, merchants and scholars, just as much as wage labourers, knew that eggs laid on Good Friday brought luck, cherished wise women able to cast a spell to prevent impotence and revered statues which, plunged into a river, brought rain within 24 hours: 'Many beliefs and practices can only be classed as transsocial phenomena, held and sustained by the entire society' (Wirth, 1984). Where reformers saw superstition or the hand of the devil, some historians have talked of 'polytheistic pagan rites left undisturbed by the superficial Christianisation of the Dark Ages' (Delumeau, 1977). Whether or not

Christianity was a mere veneer, while priests talked of sin and the hope of heaven, people seem to have thought more immediately of survival, looking to safeguard their family and community against the problems and misfortunes of life in an enchanted but dangerous universe: 'Popular religion was primarily functional, not devotional' (Monter, 1983).

Condoned for centuries, the medieval church's toleration of many such practices was initially withdrawn amid the calls of Savonarola and Erasmus for 'true piety'. But 'superstition' was a difficult subject for Catholics, especially after 1517. From the miracle of mass through the seven sacraments to wonder-working saints, Catholicism required the daily operation of the supernatural. In a failure of nerve, no new saints were canonised between 1523 and 1572. As confidence returned, a drastic pruning of miraculous relics and images began. The power to make new saints was reserved exclusively to the papacy, but priests and people heartily adopted the new shrines and cults; we must not presume blindly that clergy and people were automatic opponents. Yet however much ecclesiastical authority might try to turn the saints into exemplars of moral and religious behaviour, the people would not let go of the simultaneous hope of miraculous intervention, continuing to see them as advocates on their behalf with God, as saviours in time of crisis, as licensed wonder-workers. Philip II of Spain with his 7,000 relics was as morbid a collector of insurance policies as any medieval man. The distinction between the magical and the sacred, 'superstition' and 'true religion' was as uncertain in the minds of people then as it is among historians now.

Most customs and festivals were retained. The official mingled with the unofficial. They interacted and borrowed from one another. Paul V's *Rituale Romanum* (1614), for example, contained blessings for vines and exorcism to drive off thunder – but, then, it was much easier for Catholic reformers to be adaptable than for Protestant ones: 'If the people were going to resort to magic anyway, it was far better that it should be a magic over which the church maintained some control' (Thomas, 1971). Reforming zeal might be intolerant, but not all clergy were zealous and reform decrees were implemented haphazardly. The offensive against popular religion may belong with initiatives to regulate alehouses and carnivals on the agenda of 'a coalition of clerical and lay ruling elites' (Po-Chia Hsia, 1989) working to reverse a perceived collapse in morality and to stem a perceived rising tide of disorder. But the taming process was not just one way. If the pull of communal loyalties or individual fears were enough to draw 17th-century German Protestants to neighbouring Catholic shrines, the vigorous survival of local religious commitments in Catholic lands should not surprise: 'The local landscape had a sacred overlay of special places for contacting the divine' (Christian, 1981). In some parishes it was the laity who held the rights to organise festivals and dismiss their priest. As the people were not necessarily defenceless so the clergy were not in perpetual conflict with their parishes. Catholic practice was supple. Priests 'understood the need to accommodate themselves to the community around them, whatever the bishop might want' (Forster, 1992). Pilgrimages, rosaries, blessings and exorcisms mingled with the spells and cures of folklore. Shorn of excess, local religion with its deep sense of sacred objects and rites was strengthened. Tridentine approval of images, relics and saints guaranteed it, and kept churches full.

7.1   Official definitions of superstition

7.1(a)

It is superstitious to expect any effect from anything when that effect cannot be produced by natural causes, divine action or the church's authority ... A practice may seem innocent, even blameless, because it is associated with Scriptural sentences, crosses, blessings, giving of alms or other holy things. The more that superstition is accompanied by holy things, the more criminal it is, even if   5 covered by tradition or ancient authority.

Decree of the Council of Malines, 1607, in J-B. Thiers, *Traicté des superstitions*, Paris, 1679, II, pp. 8, 14†

7.1(b)

I hold that some images of Our Lady that worked many miracles in the past do so no longer in punishment for our inordinate self-interest and avarice; for hardly has a holy image begun to be known for a miracle when within two days the walls are covered with shrouds, crutches, hands and feet of wax,[1] without any more justification or legal testimony than the avarice of those who commit that   5 misdeed, converting to interest and lucrative commerce that which should be used to incite the devotion of the faithful. The holy Council of Trent was well aware of this danger, which it sought to preclude by so justly ordaining that no new miracle be admitted without judicial and rigorous episcopal investigation.

[1] Offerings representing the miraculous cure of a limb.

Pedro Navarro, Jesuit theologian, 1622, quoted in W. A. Christian, *Local Religion in Sixteenth-Century Spain*, Princeton University Press, Princeton, 1981, p. 247

7.2   Officially approved rites

7.2(a)   Protection from plague

[The Bishop] blessed water in which he dipped a bone of St Columba and sent it for the sick to drink. Many partook and were made whole. But one pert fellow answered 'Why sends the bishop water for us to drink? I had rather he had sent the best of his ale.' That man perished of the plague with the rest that did not receive the water of St Columba.

Bishop Brown of Dunkeld, 1500, in J. Macqueen, 'Alexander Myln, Bishop George Brown and the Chapter of Dunkeld', *Studies in Church History,* *Subsidia 8,* **Ecclesiastical History Society, Basil Blackwell Publishers, Oxford, 1991, p. 353**

7.2(b)   Baptism

At the church door, the priest makes over the baby an exorcism, after this manner: First he blows upon the baby in token that the evil spirit by the power of God shall be expelled ... Third, the priest puts salt in the baby's mouth, which betokens that his words should ever be seasoned with the spiritual salt of wisdom ... Sixth, the priest takes his spittle and anoints the baby's nostrils and ears, to   5 signify that a Christian should have a good name ... [and] have always his ears open to the word of God.

The Catechism of John Hamilton, Archbishop of St Andrew's, 1552, **ed. T. G. Law, Oxford, 1884, pp. 189–90**

7.3   Veneration of a prospective saint: Francis de Sales

His heart was taken to our Visitation at Lyons itself where it is now kept with great reverence in a silver case the shape of a heart. It looks fresh, red and soft, and it exudes a certain liquid rather like oil which soaks the fine silk in which the heart is kept folded. This often has to be changed for giving away to people who ask for it and receive it reverently ... People touch rosaries against the coffin, also   5 linen cloths for laying on the sick ... This great veneration goes on and increases every day so that our church which was never crowded in the past and only had one daily Mass said in it, is now so full that it cannot hold all the people who want to get in; and often they have to queue outside ... It simply isn't possible to describe the great tenderness and never ending devotion which people show at   10 this tomb: some kiss it, some lay their heads against it, others rest their arm or leg there, or whatever hurts. They scrape the stone of the tomb and reverently keep the dust that comes away.

Francis de Sales died in 1622 and was canonised in 1665.

St Chantal, 1627, in *St Francis de Sales, a Testimony,* **ed. E. Stopp, Faber & Faber, London, 1967, pp. 155–9**

Questions

1 (a) Why is **7.1(b)** suspicious of 'new miracles' **[line 9]**?
  (b) Judged by **7.1(a)**, might post-Tridentine regulations have condemned **7.2(a)** and **7.2(b)**? Explain your answer.
2 'Relics were the cutting edge of a massive physical presence of the supernatural' (Galpern, *The Religions of the People in Sixteenth-Century Champagne*, 1976).
  (i) What did the pilgrims in **7.3** want?
  (ii) Consider and explain how **7.1(b)** would have reacted to **7.3**.
  (iii) How does **7.2(a)** help us to understand the behaviour reported in the last sentence of **7.3**?
3 'The Catholic Church's concept of superstition always had a certain elasticity about it' (Thomas, *Religion and the Decline of Magic*, 1971). Do **7.1–7.3** confirm that to be true? Justify your answer.

7.4 The people and their saints: contract with the divine

We witnessed a great drought in this town, and after many processions were made to the chapels on the outskirts ... considering the dryness of the township, and that everything was being ruined as it was already April, almost all of the people of the town decided to go [to the shrine of Our Lady] in procession one morning, including a great number of men, women and children and some 5
brothers of the Holy True Cross who went flagellating themselves. All of these people, together with the clergy, left the town under calm skies ... [At the shrine] they celebrated mass and preached and then left to return to the town. And it pleased Our Lord through the intercession of this Holy Lady Saint His Mother to send so much rain that everyone got wet and had to return very quickly 10
because the roads turned to rivers. As a result all of the townspeople held it certain that this grace and many others in remedy of the needs of this town had been done through the intercession of this Holy Lady.

Testimony of the town of Chillón, 1579, in Christian, *Local Religion*, p. 64

7.5 Popular assumptions

At dusk [9 November 1579], it began to rain very heavily and there was terrible thunder and lightning. Three men from Valence were in Croix-la-Valleau when the lightning started. At once, two crossed themselves, but the third mocked them, saying 'You pray too sweetly. The devil will not take you.' But at that very moment, the blasphemer was struck dead by the lightning, the others being 5
totally unharmed. The dead man was said to be a Huguenot ... This only goes to show how great a shield is the sign of the cross.

Mémoires de Eustache Piémond, **ed. J. B. Durand, Paris, 1885, p. 85†**

7.6   The parish triumphs over its priest

The Sunday after Easter [1579], the people of Courlons asked their priest to
make a procession to the church of Sergines to petition God for the preservation
of the fruits of the earth during the present heavy frosts. The priest agreed, but
said they should go to Serbonnes which was closer ... After vespers, the whole
parish made the procession, led by the priest and the cross ... Outside the village,   5
the people took the road to the church of their choice. When the priest saw
himself held in contempt, he stopped and began to argue with them, saying that
it could not be their decision to lead him wherever they thought best. A great
commotion soon arose. Several seized the priest and threw him into the river,
where he would have drowned had not others rescued him. While the priest was   10
being pulled from the water, the people carried on towards Sergines.

Mémoires de Claude Haton, ed. F. Bourqelot, Paris, 1857, II, p. 977†

7.7   Magic spells

The Venetian tribunal of the Holy Office has been continually employed ...
[against] the superstitious use of incantations ... Incantations were generally
accompanied by activities which made them matters for the Inquisition, i.e. the
adoration of demons, the recitation of prayers, the burning for magical purposes
of ... substances which give off sweet or foul odours. But the incantations did not   5
arise from any inclination towards heresy. Rather, they were directed towards two
ends, love and gain, which wield great power over empty-headed people.
Sometimes, indeed, love was directed towards gain, for it seemed that
incantations might be placed under the threshold of a door to instil love into
creditors and make them refrain from exacting debts. These incantations   10
produced truly diabolical results, as with those who, being at first unable to
consummate their marriages, freed themselves from impotence by urinating in the
immediate surroundings of a tomb or at the door of a church.

The papal nuncio in Venice, *c.* 1580, in Chambers and Pullan, *Venice*,
pp. 236–7

Questions

1   Why did the townsfolk in **7.4**:
    (i)   go to the Virgin Mary's shrine
    (ii) not go to her shrine straight away?
2   (a) 'The dead ... a Huguenot' **[7.5 line 6]**. Comment.
    (b) Explain the purpose of this story.
3   'Processions redrew community boundaries and reaffirmed communal
    solidarities' (Scribner, 'Cosmic Order and Daily Life', 1984). What was at
    stake in **7.6**?

4   Why were the incantations in **7.7** judged 'truly diabolical' [**line 11**]?
5   'German areas rich in pilgrimage places remained Catholic while those showing a paucity of sites embraced the Protestant faith' (Rothkrug, 'Popular Religion and Holy Shrines', 1979). Do you find that surprising? Explain your answer.
6   'The Catholic Reformation marked a second wave of Christianization in Europe far more successful in its effect than the original' (Delumeau, *Catholicism between Luther and Voltaire*, 1977). From the evidence in Chapters 6 and 7, assess the validity of that claim.

II The problem of the decline in witchcraze

To the modern eye, no early modern 'superstition' seems more alien than the witchcraze. From the late 15th to the mid 17th-century, perhaps 110,000 people were tried and 60,000 executed in a series of witchcrazes: a subject which divides historical opinion as few others. This section takes a brief overview of the eventual decline of witchcraze in Catholic territory. From the beginning, some clerics were uncertain about the reality of malevolent magic and pacts with the devil. The Inquisition in Spain in 1526 rejected the proposition that witchcraft was an illusion only by six votes to four. After the worst of Spanish witchcrazes (1610), Inquisitor Salazar declared that 'there were neither witches nor bewitched until they were talked about'. Church courts dealt with few such trials and, when they did, were known for greater clemency than civil tribunals.

How far did scepticism reflect philosophical and theological doubts about witchcraft itself, rather than legal or medical doubts sown by the poverty of evidence? Was it accidental that most early opponents of witch-hunting were Catholic? The growth of scepticism in high places was a critical development; seeds of doubt helped break the cycle. Hunting witches was infectious and, 'to the very end, arose mainly in response to rural, lower-class pressure' (Levack, 1987). Do we see here a striking example of the withdrawal of the elite from popular culture? Their view of the world certainly underwent a profound if gradual transformation. Sceptics like René Descartes (d. 1650) believed that everything should be questioned and doubted before it was accepted. The revelations of Galileo (d. 1642) and Newton (d. 1727) on the machine-like working of the universe according to fixed laws elbowed out supernatural answers to mysterious events. While some would eventually apply Descartes and Newton to doubt the existence of God, the 'clockwork universe' immediately cut the ground from under demons and, at an intellectual level, destroyed rational belief in witchcraft. Historians assert firmly, however, that the direct influence of rational scepticism and scientific advance are 'insufficient to explain the decline' (Trevor-Roper, 1967) since decline began before intellectual currents could have had any effect.

Where does that leave us? There are two possibilities particular to the Catholic world. The first lies in 'Thomism', the teachings of St Thomas Aquinas (d. 1274), which underwent a great revival in the 16th century and came to dominate the mental climate of the post-Tridentine church. Thomism asserted that the universe operated according to divinely created natural laws, which people could comprehend by reason. Further, it denied any distinction between the natural and the supernatural for everything operated according to divine authority under those universal natural laws. Within such a viewpoint, the devil had little room for movement. The second point may relate to that emphasis on personal responsibility of the individual which developed out of Trent's insistence on human co-operation with God in salvation. Individuals were masters of their own destiny and, 'as the individual's power to choose how to act was acknowledged, the visibility of the devil's role declined' (Scarre, 1987).

7.8   The testimony of an Inquisitor

I have not found even indications from which to infer that a single act of witchcraft has really occurred, whether as to going to sabbaths, being present at them, inflicting injuries, or other of the asserted facts. This enlightenment has greatly strengthened my former suspicions that the evidence of accomplices, without external proof from other parties, is insufficient to justify even arrest.   5
Moreover, my experience leads to the conviction that ... three-quarters and more have accused themselves and their accomplices falsely. I further believe that they would freely come to the Inquisition to revoke their confessions, if they thought that they would be received kindly without punishment ...

There is no need of fresh edicts ... In the diseased state of the public mind,   10
every agitation of the matter is harmful and increases the evil. I deduce the importance of silence and reserve from the experience that there were neither witches nor bewitched until they were talked and written about. This impressed me recently at Olague, near Pampeluna, where those who confessed stated that the matter started there after Fray Domingo de Sardo came there to preach about   15
these things.

Inquisitor Alonso de Salazar to the Suprema of the Inquisition, March 1612, in C. Williams, *Witchcraft*, Faber & Faber, London, 1941, pp. 252–3

7.9   The all-devouring legal machine

If now some utterance of a demoniac or some malign and idle rumour then current (for proof of the scandal is never asked) points especially to some poor and helpless Gaia, she is the first to suffer ... Therefore it is ordered that Gaia be

hauled away to prison ... If there are any who have borne her ill will, these, having now a fine opportunity to do her harm, bring against her such charges as   5
it may please them to devise ...

And so, as soon as possible, she is hurried to the torture, if indeed she has not been subjected to it on the very day of her arrest, as often happens. For in these trials there is granted to nobody an advocate or any means of fair defense, for the cry is that the crime is an excepted one, and whoever ventures to defend the   10
prisoner is brought into suspicion of the crime – as are all those who dare to utter a protest in these cases and to urge the judges to caution; for they are forthwith dubbed patrons of the witches. Thus all mouths are closed and all pens blunted ... She is, however, tortured with the torture of the first degree, i.e., the less severe. This is to be understood thus: that, although in itself it is exceeding   15
severe, yet, compared with others to follow, it is lighter. Wherefore, if she confesses, they say and noise it abroad that she has confessed without torture. Now, what prince or other dignitary who hears this can doubt that she is most certainly guilty who thus voluntarily without torture confesses her guilt? Without any scruples, therefore, after this confession she is executed. Yet she would have   20
been executed nevertheless, even though she had not confessed; for, when once a beginning has been made with the torture, the die is already cast – she cannot escape, she must die ...

If now Gaia, no matter how many times tortured, has not yet broken silence – if she contorts her features under the pain, if she loses consciousness, or the like,   25
then they cry that she is laughing or has bewitched herself ... Not only is there no door for escape, but she is compelled to accuse others, of whom she knows no ill, and whose names are not seldom suggested to her by her examiners or the executioner, or of whom she has heard as suspected or accused ... These in their turn are forced to accuse others, and these still others, and so it goes on.

Spee wrote the *Cautio* after serving as confessor to condemned witches in Würzburg, 1627–9.

Friedrich Spee, Jesuit priest, *Cautio Criminalis*, 1631, in G. L. Burr, *The Witch Persecutions*, New York, 1889, pp. 31–5

7.10 Gentlemen sceptics

7.10(a) 'It is better to lean toward doubt'

I am plain and rude, and stick to the main point, and that which is more likely, avoiding those ancient reproaches: *Men are most apt to believe what they least understand;* and *through the lust of human wit, obscure things are more easily credited.* I see very well that men are angry, and that I am forbidden to doubt upon pain of execrable injuries. A new way of persuading! ... Let us not seek illusions from   5 without and unknown, we who are perpetually agitated with illusions domestic and our own.

Methinks a man is pardonable in disbelieving a miracle, as much at least as he can divert and elude the verification by no wonderful ways. And I am of St Augustine's opinion, that 'tis better to lean towards doubt than assurance in   10
things hard to prove and dangerous to believe ... After all, 'tis setting a man's conjectures at a very high price to cause a man to be roasted alive.

Montaigne, 'Of Cripples', 1588, in *The Essays of Michel de Montaigne*, **tr. C. Cotton, London, 1875, pp. 821–3**

7.10(b) The power of reason

Reason alone is my ruler, to whom I voluntarily pay homage ... Do not embrace an opinion because many people hold it ... A philosopher ought to judge the crowd, and not judge like the crowd ...

I have almost never been told a story about Witches that did not ordinarily take place three or four hundred leagues away. This remoteness made me suspect   5
that they wanted to deprive the listener of the desire and power to learn about it himself. In addition, this band of men dressed as cats is located in the middle of the countryside, without witnesses. The Faith of one person alone should be suspect in such a miraculous thing. Close to a village, it is easier to deceive idiots. The woman was poor and old. She was poor: necessity might have constrained   10
her to lie for money. She was old: age had weakened her reason. Age makes one gossipy: she invented this story to amuse her neighbors. Age weakens the sight: she mistook a Hare for a Cat ... It is more likely that something happened which is seen every day and not a supernatural adventure, without logic or precedent. If you please, examine one of these captured Witches. You will find that he is a   15
very crass Peasant ... I am not yet convinced nor obliged to believe that it is the Devil who does all this monkey business ... If the Devils are forced, as you say, to perform miracles in order to illumine us, let them do convincing ones. Let them take the towers of Notre Dame of Paris, where there are so many unbelievers, and carry them unbroken into the countryside of Saint-Denis to   20
dance a Spanish sarabande.

Cyrano de Bergerac, *A Letter against Witches*, **1654, in** *European Witchcraft*, **ed. E. W. Monter, Random House/Knopf, New York, 1969, pp. 114–20**

Questions

1   'Salazar's memorandum was not a victory for rationalism but quite simply for the laws of evidence' (Kamen, *Inquisition and Society in Spain in the 16th and 17th Centuries*, 1985). Do you agree? Justify your answer.

2   Summarise Spee's attitude in **7.9** to:
   (i)   accusations of witchcraft
   (ii) the role of torture.
3   What do **7.8** and **7.9** tell us about attitudes among the Catholic clergy to witchcraft?
4   (a)   Are the witchcraze doubts in **7.10(b)** related to the writer's attitude to peasants?
     (b)   Explain the relevance of 'reason' to the doubts expressed in **7.10(a)** and **(b)**.
5   From **4.6** and the table on page 18, suggest why post-Tridentine salvation theology might have helped undermine belief in witchcraft among Catholics.

III   The problem of slavery in Spanish America

The age of discovery quickly became an age of empire. Unlike the Portuguese, the Spanish operated a 'carefully formulated and clearly enunciated policy of conquest and territorial dominance' (Villiers, 1987). Thus it was the Spanish empire in which controversy erupted over the status of conquered peoples, but why? Medieval Christendom enslaved Muslims whilst crusading; nobody objected. Feudal servitude, effectively the equivalent of slavery, was common across much of Europe. The surprising thing is not that Europeans applied this familiar economic institution to sustain colonial societies, but that some demurred. More puzzling still, those who struggled to protect American Indians rarely noticed (before the 17th century) the Portuguese use of negro slavery.

Europeans in the 16th century remade the world in their own image, exporting their values and expectations to the new lands. Those who found savages did so because they expected to find them; likewise those who discovered Arcadia or the Garden of Eden. To reform-minded friars busily denouncing the wickedness of late medieval Christendom, yearning for lost innocence and proclaiming the impending apocalypse, the naked simplicity and honesty of the Arawaks encountered by Columbus seemed the long-awaited sign. In a spotless new world, pure Christianity would be re-founded. It proved a compelling fantasy and the early years of mission had about them 'an unmatched euphoric quality' (Cervantes, 1970). The myth of innocence devoured by the sinful corruption of the old world would be more powerful still. Before their eyes, the friars saw paradise destroyed by the rapacity of the conquistadores.

Since America was the first entirely new world with which Europeans had

to come to terms, it was America which provoked debate on the humanity
of its inhabitants. All were clearly 'heathen'. Some were classed 'savage',
others 'barbarian', but the terms were interchangeable. More significant was
the question of whether they were humans in a primitive state, no different
to pagan Europeans before conversion, or whether they were humans in an
inferior, degenerate state caused by the sin of their ancestors and thus,
according to Aristotle, 'natural slaves'. Among champions of Indian rights,
pride of place belongs to Bartolomé de Las Casas (d. 1566), the slave-
owning adventurer who renounced his past, joined the Dominican friars and
became the most prolific writer and preacher in the abolitionist cause. His
prime target in the assault on the greed and immorality of colonial society
was the *encomienda*, a system of forced labour in the fields and mines central
to the economic development of Spanish America. To attack it was to question the nature of Spanish dominion. But for campaigning priests, the
Indians had acquired the full status of Castilian subjects upon conquest. The
encomienda thus imposed a tyranny which abused their legal liberties and
tarnished the repute of Spain.

Dominicans and Jesuits were energetic Thomists and as such took it upon
themselves 'to refute all the heretics of this present age' (Cardinal
Bellarmine, 1593). They had more than Protestants in their sights. Equally
dangerous, Thomists argued, were certain humanist political ideas. One was
Machiavelli's doctrine that 'for the benefit of the state, rulers may use any
means, good or bad, just or unjust' (*The Prince*, 1513). Conquistador behaviour seemed the amoral politics of Machiavelli at work, and that threatened
the foundations of Christian society. Another was the proposition that
genuine communities could only be based on godliness. When applied to
empire, that provided a neat defence for slavery for it meant that pagans possessed no genuine dominion over their lands. Such an idea ran counter to the
Thomist insistence that all people possessed the inherent ability to see and
follow universal laws of nature 'which God has inscribed in their hearts'
(Francisco de Vitoria, *c.* 1535). Rooted in the same conviction which led
them to champion so vigorously at Trent the doctrine of inherent justice in
the great debates over justification, it led them to fight slavery in America:
'In their view of the capacity of man, the conquistadores had made the same
mistake as Luther' (Skinner, 1978).

7.11 'These little men'

Because the Indians live under a form of government does not prove they are
equal to the Spanish. All it proves is that they are not monkeys and not totally
devoid of the capacity to reason ... Look at them and you will see they have no

laws, no science, no letters, keep no memorials to their history (save vague and obscure stories). They even lack private property ... At the same time, they   5
indulge in human sacrifices to false idols and hold disgusting feasts to eat that flesh ... Who could doubt that these little men, so barbaric, so impious, so obscene are as different from the Spanish as children are to adults and as women are to men? ...

   If an act is performed cruelly by unjust men, and I have heard that the war in   10
the Indies has been waged with the cruelty of barbarians and the style of bandits, that does not undermine the legitimate claims of the prince who authorised it ... Natural law can be found only among civilised nations who, compared with the uncivilised, are as a lord is to a peasant for, as the peasant is by nature in service to his lord, so the uncivilised by nature require (in their own interest) the   15
authority of civilised princes if they are to learn the Christian religion and good morals, customs and a better way of life ... So, let the Indians be divided among just and honourable Spaniards.

Juan de Sepúlveda, *Democrates alter*, 1547, *Boletin de la real academia de historia*, XXI, Madrid, 1892, pp. 284–325 †

7.12   Natural servitude: a biological justification

The Indians can be said to be slaves of the Spaniards ... in accordance with the doctrine of Aristotle's *Politics* that those who need to be ruled and governed by others may be called their slaves ... And for this reason Nature specially proportioned their bodies, so that they should have the strength for personal service. The Spaniards, on the other hand, are delicately proportioned, and were   5
made prudent and clever, so that they should be able to lead a political and civil life.

From a memorandum by mine owners in New Spain to Philip III, 1600, in J. H. Elliott, *The Old World and the New, 1492–1650*, Cambridge University Press, 1970, p. 44

7.13   Limitations on dominion and slavery

1. Whether Our Most Christian King may govern the Indians despotically or tyrannically

Answer: It is not just for Christian Princes to make war on infidels because of a desire to dominate or for their wealth, but only to spread the faith. Therefore, if the inhabitants of those lands never before Christianized wish to listen to and   5
receive the faith, Christian Princes may not invade their territory ...

2. Whether the King may exercise over them political dominion

Answer: If an invitation to accept Christianity has not been made, the infidels may justly defend themselves even though the King, moved by Christian zeal and supported by papal authority, has waged just war. Such infidels may not be held   10
as slaves unless they pertinaciously deny obedience to the prince or refuse to accept Christianity.

Matiás de Paz, Dominican and professor of theology at Valladolid University, to King Ferdinand, 1512, in L. Hanke, *The Spanish Struggle for Justice in the Conquest of America,* **University of Pennsylvania Press, Philadelphia, 1949, pp. 27–8**

7.14 'All men are natural masters'

The Spanish were bound to use force of arms to continue their work of conversion, but I fear they adopted measures in excess of what is allowed by human and divine law ... Among all men there is an equal ability to found their own governments, whether they be Christian or not, which means that all men are natural masters. Therefore even if the Christian faith has been announced to   5
the barbarians with complete and sufficient arguments and they have still refused to receive it, this does not supply a legitimate reason for making war on them. Those barbarians cannot be barred from being true owners, alike in public and private war, by reason of the sin of unbelief or any other mortal sin; nor does such sin entitle Christians to seize their goods and lands for they possess true   10
dominion ... If they seem intelligent or stupid, I attribute it to their barbarous upbringing. Even among ourselves we find many peasants who differ little from brutes.

Francisco de Vitoria, Dominican and professor of theology at Salamanca University, *De Indis,* **written 1532–9, first published 1557, ed. E. Nys, Carnegie Institution, Washington DC, 1917, pp. 120–35**

7.15 A preacher attacks colonists

In order to make your sins against the Indians known to you I have come up on this pulpit, I who am a Voice of Christ crying in the wilderness of this island ... Why do you keep them so oppressed and weary, not giving them enough to eat nor taking care of them in their illnesses? For with the excessive work you demand of them they fall ill and die, or rather you kill them with your desire to   5
extract and acquire gold every day ... Are those not men? Have they not rational souls? Are you not bound to love them as you love yourselves? Be certain that, in such a state as this, you can no more be saved than the Moors or Turks.

Antonio de Montesinos, a Dominican in Hispaniola, 1511, in Sir A. Helps, *The Spanish Conquest in America,* **London, 1900, I, p. 176**

7.16 'The Indians are truly men'

The sublime God so loved the human race that He created man in such wise that
he might participate, not only in the good that other creatures enjoy, but
endowed him with capacity to attain to the inaccessible and invisible Supreme
Good and behold it face to face ... [Inspired by the Devil] his satellites have
published abroad that the Indians of the West and the South, and other people of   5
whom We have recent knowledge should be treated as dumb brutes created for
our service, pretending that they are incapable of receiving the Catholic faith ...
[But] the Indians are truly men and they are not only capable of understanding
the Catholic faith but, according to our information, they desire exceedingly to
receive it. Desiring to provide ample remedy for these evils, we define and   10
declare ... notwithstanding whatever may be said to the contrary, the said Indians
and all other people who may later be discovered by Christians, are by no means
to be deprived of their liberty or the possession of their property, even though
they be outside the faith of Jesus.

Sublimis Deus, **bull of Paul III, June 1537, in F. MacNutt,** *Bartholomew de*
Las Casas, **G. P. Putnam, New York, 1909, pp. 427–31**

7.17 Las Casas creates the 'Black Legend'

The Spaniards entered like wolves, tigers and lions which had been starving for
many days, and since forty years they have done nothing else ... [Hispaniola] was
the first to be destroyed and made into a desert. The Christians began by taking
the women and children, to use and to abuse them, and to eat of the substance of
their toil and labour, instead of contenting themselves with what the Indians gave   5
them spontaneously, according to the means of each. Such stores are always
small; because they keep no more than they ordinarily need, which they acquire
with little labour; but what is enough for three households, of ten persons each,
for a month, a Christian eats and destroys in one day ...

   The Christians, with their horses and swords and lances, began to slaughter   10
and practise strange cruelty among them ... They made bets as to who would slit
a man in two, or cut off his head at one blow: or they opened up his bowels.
They tore the babes from their mothers' breast by the feet, and dashed their
heads against the rocks. Others they seized by the shoulders and threw into the
rivers, laughing and joking ... They made a gallows just high enough for the feet   15
to nearly touch the ground, and by thirteens, in honour and reverence of our
Redeemer and the twelve Apostles, they put wood underneath and, with fire, they
burned the Indians alive. They wrapped the bodies of others in dry straw, binding
them in it and setting fire to it; and so they burned them. They cut off the hands
of all they wished taken alive, made them carry them fastened on to them, and   20
said: 'Go and carry letters': that is, take the news to those who have fled ...

   [In Cuba,[1] Prince Hatuey] was taken and they burnt him alive ... When he was
tied to the stake, a Franciscan, a holy man, who was there, spoke as much as he

could to him of the teachings of our faith, of which he had never before heard ... After thinking a little, Hatuey asked the monk whether the Christians went to heaven; the monk answered that those who were good went there. The prince at once said, without any more thought, that he did not wish to go there, but rather to hell so as not to be where the Spaniards were ...   25

I was induced to write this work ... that God may not destroy my fatherland Castile for such great sins ... I have great hope for the Emperor and King is getting to understand the wickedness and treachery that, contrary to the will of God and himself, is and has been done to these peoples; heretofore the truth has been studiously hidden from him ... by these tyrants who, under pretext that they are serving the King, dishonour God, and rob and destroy the King.   30

[1] The young Las Casas was a member of the 1511 Cuba expedition.

A Short Account of the Destruction of the Indies, written 1542, first published 1552, in MacNutt, *Las Casas*, pp. 315, 318–20, 330, 411–12, 414

Questions

1   (a) By what criteria do **7.11** and **7.12** judge Indians to be natural slaves?
    (b) How does **7.12** reflect the needs of its authors?
2   Consider how far **7.13** and **7.14** are in agreement on Indian rights. What does **7.15** add?
3   How does **7.11** envisage Indians will be Christianised? To what extent do **7.13**, **7.14** and **7.16** disagree?
4   (a) In what ways does **7.16** show Thomist influence?
    (b) Why were Dominicans so prominent in this campaign?
5   (a) Suggest reasons why **7.17** goes into such graphic detail.
    (b) How does **7.13** reveal the purpose of the story of Hatuey?
    (c) From **7.11–7.16**, set out in parallel columns the grounds upon which Spanish attitudes and behaviour in **7.17** would have been (i) defended, (ii) denounced.
    (d) What is Las Casas' purpose in the final paragraph?
6   Do you consider the defence of Indian rights an example of reformed Catholicism in action? Justify your answer.

Summary

'The ambition utterly to revise the basic principles behind peoples' dealings with their God, their cosmos and their predicament was a piece of intellectual imperialism of colossal proportions' (Cameron, *The European Reformation*, 1991).

Assess this statement by the evidence in Chapter 7.

References

F. Cervantes, *Life in the Imperial and Loyal City of Mexico in New Spain*, Greenwood Press, Greenwood, 1970

A. Galpern, *The Religions of the People in Sixteenth-Century Champagne*, Harvard University Press, 1976

B. Levack, *The Witch-Hunt in Early Modern Europe*, Longman, 1987

E. Monter, *Ritual, Myth and Magic in Early Modern Europe*, Harvester, 1983

L. Rothkrug, 'Popular Religion and Holy Shrines', in *Religion and the People, 800–1700*, ed. J. Obelkevich, University of North Carolina Press, 1979

G. Scarre, *Witchcraft and Magic in Sixteenth and Seventeenth Century Europe*, Macmillan, 1987

R. Scribner, 'Cosmic Order and Daily Life', in his *Popular Culture and Popular Movements in Reformation Germany*, Hambledon Press, 1987

Q. Skinner, *The Foundations of Modern Political Thought: The Age of the Reformation*, Cambridge University Press, 1978

K. Thomas, *Religion and the Decline of Magic*, Weidenfeld, 1971

H. R. Trevor-Roper, 'The European Witch-craze', in his *Religion, the Reformation and Social Change*, Macmillan, 1967

J. Villiers, 'Portuguese Malacca and Spanish Manila: two concepts of Empire', in *Portuguese Asia*, ed. R. Ptak, Steiner Wiesbaden, Stuttgart, 1987

J. Wirth, 'Against the Acculturation Thesis', in *Religion and Society in Early Modern Europe, 1500–1800* ed. K. von Greyerz, George Allen & Unwin, 1984

For Cameron, Christian, Delumeau, Forster, Po-Chia Hsia, Kamen (1985) and Scribner (1984) see *Suggestions for further reading*.

8 Fire and sword: four studies in Counter Reformation

The tide had been running against Rome. Between 1530 and 1546, 13 German states became Lutheran, including two electorates. During those same years, the Scandinavian kingdoms, Transylvania and England also quit the Roman fold, while Protestantism made significant headway in Lithuania, Poland, Hungary and France. The prospects seemed so poor around 1540 that it would not have been far-fetched to suggest Catholicism would survive only around the Mediterranean, in Portugal, the Habsburg lands, Bavaria and Ireland. Well, that did not happen. The church recovered its nerve and went on to recover much lost territory. This final chapter investigates some of the ways in which priests, popes and princes marched out to join battle with heresy. Church and state were by no means always in agreement over what to do or how to do it; neither side in the Reformation conflict was that united. Territorial and diplomatic interests kept Catholic states from uniting in a grand coalition against Protestantism. Revived claims of papal jurisdiction sent Catholic monarchs scurrying to defend privileges over the church in their kingdoms won by their ancestors. But decisions taken in the 1540s to reject any understanding with the Protestants meant that the Counter Reformation could begin. Christendom plunged into ideological conflict.

I The Index, the Inquisition and Spanish Protestantism

Nothing symbolises the traditional image of Counter Reformation better than the burning of books and heretics. Historians of late have tried to look beyond martyrs, refugees and intolerance to assess dispassionately such (to us) foul instruments of policy. This is a topic which, more than most, demands effort on our part to understand the values of another world. Heresy was seen as coming from the devil, a contagion needing drastic surgery if its spread was to be halted. In the middle of an ideologically based war, the pursuit of learning and freedom of belief would have seemed not merely foolish but ideas as dangerous as heresy itself – which was why Protestants also burned their opponents and their writings.

Censorship predated both Protestantism and printing, but the Protestants' skilled use of propaganda demanded firm action. No centralised action was taken, however, until Paul IV in 1559 introduced an *Index librorum prohibitorum* listing books to be banned across Christendom. Several states were reluctant to accept it, seeing yet another attempt to infringe their sovereignty. But their primary purpose in maintaining their own censorship was to tailor it to their own requirements. The Spanish Index of 1559, for example, should be seen not so much as a rival to the pope's as the culmination of 30 years' work to keep the country orthodox and as a specific response to the discovery of Protestants in 1557–8. Minds closed and attitudes hardened earlier in Spain than anywhere.

Spanish inquisitors looked on any private expression of religion as suspect and from 1525 hunted *alumbrados* – lay groups who met to read the Bible and pray in search of a pure, inner devotion. The import of all foreign books was banned. Attendance at foreign universities was forbidden. Spain turned itself into 'a citadel barred against the outer world' (Elliott, 1963), a curious mentality for a superpower. Catholicism was still on the defensive. Censorship was tighter than anything found among Protestants and 'moved steadily from the selective to the general' (Haliczer, 1990).

8.1   The folly of toleration

[If the prince] pretend to favor both sides, he will be suspected by both and, remaining in the centre, he will get the favor of neither, but will engender the hate of all and ... trying to keep both seats, will tumble to the ground from both ... The wife will turn away from her own husband as impious. The husband will impute the crime of adultery to his wife who without consulting him goes to   5
the meeting of another religion ... For to what other end will this ungodly lack of restraint tend by which the mob is freed from all fear unless that, after the church has been violated, the clergy prostrate, and individual churches seized and burned, the blaze spreads like a serpent more widely and takes in the laying low of the nobles? ... The day that gives freedom of worship puts an end to the   10
happiness of the Commonwealth, and the name of liberty, bright in aspect and title, which in all history has seduced many a man, is to be found in fact false and empty.

Juan de Mariana, a Jesuit, *De Rege*, 1605, in G. Lewy, *Constitutionalism and Statecraft during the Golden Age of Spain: A Study of the Political Philosophy of Juan de Mariana*, Librairie Droz, Geneva, 1960, pp. 89–90

8.2   Tridentine controls over printing

[Because printers] print without the permission of ecclesiastical superiors the
books of the Holy Scriptures and the notes and commentaries thereon of all
persons indiscriminately, often with the name of the press omitted, often also
under a fictitious press-name, and what is worse, without the name of the
author ... it shall not be lawful for anyone to print or to have printed any books   5
whatsoever dealing with sacred doctrinal matters without the name of the author,
or in the future to sell them, or even to have them in possession, unless they
have first been examined and approved ... The approbation of such books shall be
given in writing and shall appear authentically at the beginning of the book,
whether written or printed.

Decree of the Council of Trent, April 1546, in Schroeder, *Canons and
Decrees,* **p. 19**

8.3   Censorship in Spain

8.3(a)

No bookseller, book dealer or other of whatever condition shall henceforth carry,
bring, smuggle, possess or sell any book, printed or in manuscript, in any
language, which has been forbidden to the Christian faithful by the office of the
Inquisition, upon pain of death and the confiscation of all goods, lands and
possessions.

**Decree of Juana, Regent in Spain, September 1558, in A. Rumeau de
Armas,** *Historia de la censura literaria gubernativa en España,* **Madrid, 1940,
p. 41†**

8.3(b)

The faint-hearted have reacted by becoming more faint-hearted and those
dedicated to virtue are in dismay, seeing that the Inquisitor-General has
published an edict forbidding almost all the books in Spanish that have been used
up to now by those who try to serve God; and we are in times when women are
told to stick to their beads[1] and not bother about other devotions.

[1] 'their beads' = the rosary.

An unnamed Jesuit, September 1559, in H. Kamen, *Inquisition and Society
in Spain in the Sixteenth and Seventeenth Centuries,* **Weidenfeld &
Nicolson, London, 1985, pp. 90–1**

Questions

1   Why should **8.1** talk of the commonwealth rather than the devil?
2   (a)   What does **8.2** reveal about recent problems with censorship?
    (b)   Did this decree ban vernacular Bibles and religious literature [**see 4.5**]?
3   Consider why **8.3(a)** was successful whereas **3.6** and **3.7** were not.
4   'Hold fast daughters. Their lists cannot take away the Our Father and Hail Mary' (St Teresa of Avila, *c.* 1564). Explain the anger in **8.3(b)**.

The Inquisition

Throughout the 16th century, the Inquisition in Spain prosecuted under 400 alleged Protestants, of whom 70 per cent were foreigners. To deduce therefore that Protestantism only ever secured a minute following would be to miss the point. Spain witnessed one of the most effective of Counter Reformation campaigns. The Inquisition systematically burned and strangled Protestantism out of existence. First it pursued *alumbrados* and the disciples of Erasmus, convinced that both were at least embryonic Lutherans. Then in 1557–8, several small groups of Protestants were uncovered. The shock of that discovery cannot be exaggerated. Neither can the savage persecution that it unleashed.

The Protestant scare contributed substantially to an incipient suspicion of everything foreign and an all-consuming paranoia: Spain was in danger. Nobody was safe. The student St Ignatius Loyola was investigated. St Teresa of Avila had to be extremely careful: the *alumbrados* legacy made inquisitors especially suspicious of women. The most extraordinary victim was Bartolomé de Carranza (d. 1576), Archbishop of Toledo, who spent 17 years in Inquisition cells. Although eventually declared innocent of Protestantism, he never cleared his name. Neither the king nor the pope could help him; in fact, he became the pawn in a bitter test of strength between Madrid and Rome over who would try him. This 'festering scandal' (Monter, 1990) reveals much. Philip II saw in the Inquisition a means to strengthen his grip on the state and to keep it heresy-free. Crown and Inquisition grew together, but the instrument created was so powerful that none could control it. Popular in Castile, it was seen in the rest of the Spanish empire as the instrument of Castilian domination, of Spanish oppression. In the early stages of Dutch revolt, only a hatred of the Inquisition bound Catholic and Protestant together. Modern studies may stress 'the gap between what it professed and what it actually put into practice' (Kamen, 1988), and point out that 'contemporary secular legal systems punished their prisoners more severely than the Inquisition' (Monter, 1990). Nonetheless, the extermination of Spain's Protestants stands proof of its deadly effectiveness.

8.4   Spain in danger

Since this affair is more important for the service of Our Lord and the good and preservation of these realms than any other, and since it is only in its beginnings, with such small forces that they can be easily put down, it is necessary to place the greatest stress and weight on a quick remedy and exemplary punishment. I do not know whether it will be enough in these cases to follow the usual practice, by which according to common law all those who beg for mercy and have their confession accepted are pardoned with a light penance if it is a first offence. Such people, if set free, are at liberty to commit the same offence, particularly if they are educated persons ...   5

It is clear that they cannot act without armed organisation and leaders, and so it must be seen whether they can be proceeded against as creators of sedition, upheaval, riots and disturbance in the state; they would then be guilty of rebellion and could not expect any mercy ... [In Flanders] I wanted to introduce an Inquisition to punish the heresies that some people had caught from neighbouring Germany and England and even France. Everyone opposed this on the grounds that there were no Jews among them. Finally an order was issued declaring that all people of whatever state and condition who came under certain specified categories were to be *ipso facto* burnt and their goods confiscated. Necessity obliged me to act in this way.   10   15

Charles V to Juana, Regent in Spain, May 1558, in H. Lea, *A History of the Inquisition in Spain*, Macmillan, New York, 1906, III, pp. 434–5

8.5   The Inquisition and the Crown

8.5(a)

It is true that the Inquisition intervenes in all affairs, regardless of rank or status. It is the real Lord who rules and reigns over Spain.

From a despatch of the Venetian ambassador in Madrid, 1565, in E. Alberi, *Relazione degli Ambasciatori Veneti al Senato*, Florence, 1846, IX, p. 158†

8.5(b)

Article 5: Outside cases of heresy, inquisitors must not interfere with the execution of justice by royal judges under pretext that culprits have committed offences pertaining to them, but in such cases the judges shall be allowed to execute justice ...

Article 8: Inquisitors are not to publish edicts with excommunication for the discovery of debts, thefts or other hidden offences committed against officials.

Article 9: Persons arrested, except for heresy, are not to be confined in the secret prison but in the public one, where they can confer with their counsel ...

Article 10: Inquisitors shall not give safe-conducts to persons outlawed or banished by the royal judges, except in cases of heresy.

Agreement between the Cortes and the Inquisition in Valencia, 1568, in Lea, *A History of the Inquisition*, I, pp. 443–4

8.6   Long shadows

8.6(a)   An Erasmian prosecuted

Maria de Cazalla, teacher and dogmatizer of *alumbrados*, preached to them in public and indoctrinated them, quoting for this purpose sacred authorities and psalms from the Holy Scriptures and declaring this to them in the vernacular ... Many persons went to hear her and they listened to her as a preacher, which was scandalous for the people, since she cannot and should not preach, being a woman.

From a trial in 1532, in Weber, *Teresa of Avila*, p. 28

8.6(b)   St Ignatius imprisoned

I was arrested and kept in custody for forty-two days. The same thing took place in Salamanca, where I was not only confined to jail but also put into chains for twenty-two days ... There was never any question of being involved with schismatics or Lutherans or *alumbrados* for I never knew any of them or had anything to do with them ... [The reason] was that I, being without education, should venture to speak at such length on spiritual subjects.

Ignatius to King John III of Portugal, March 1545, in *Letters of St Ignatius of Loyola*, tr. W. Young, Loyola University Press, Chicago, 1959, pp. 80–1

8.6(c)   St Teresa accused

That learned men should come to learn from a woman and recognize her as a leader in matters of prayer and spiritual doctrine ... is an argument for the novelty of this doctrine ... It is nothing new for women of erroneous life and doctrine to deceive wise and eminent men.

From one of five charges of heresy brought against St Teresa, 1589–91, in Weber, *Teresa of Avila*, p. 160

8.6(d)   Teresa's method of self-defence

I don't know if I'm guessing right in what I say, for although I have heard this [biblical] story about Jacob, I don't know if I'm remembering it correctly ...

It should be remembered that the weakness of our nature is very great, especially in women, and that it shows itself most markedly in this way of prayer; so it is essential that we should not at once suppose every little imagining of ours   5
to be a vision ...

In difficult matters, even though it seems to me I understand and that I speak the truth, I always use this expression 'it seems to me'.

Extracts from her writings, in Weber, *Teresa of Avila*, pp. 106–7, 145

8.7   Archbishop Carranza's heresy

8.7(a)

[The devout laity are able to read the Bible] better than those who know Latin and other languages. I don't say this because the sciences that God has communicated to men do not have their place in the Scriptures, but because the Holy Spirit has His disciples and illumines them and gives them help ... [I] certify that with my advice some people have read the Holy Scriptures and this   5
has helped them live a better life. These included some women.

***Commentary on the Christian Catechism*, 1558, in Weber, *Teresa of Avila*, p. 30**

8.7(b)

In this [penance], both extremes are at fault; only the middle ground is safe. The new heretics follow one extreme and say that penance is to be found in faith alone and in the contrition of sin. The other is followed by many Catholics who put all their contrition into confessing to a priest.

Sermon before the King and Queen, London, March 1555, in J. I. Tellechea Idígoras, *Fray Bartolomé Carranza y el Cardenal Pole: Un Navarro en la Restauracion Católica de Inglaterra, 1554–1558*, Pamplona, 1977, p. 323†

Questions

1   (a)   Explain the reference to Jews in **8.4 line 16**.
    (b)   What in **8.4** seems to have been Charles' chief anxiety?
2   Do the dates of **8.3(a)**, **8.3(b)** and **8.4** explain their severity?

3   (a) What impression of the Inquisition does **8.5(b)** give?
    (b) Philip II declared this agreement void. Comment.
4   Why were St Ignatius [**8.6(b)**] and St Teresa [**8.6(c)**] suspected of heresy?
5   What do you make of St Teresa's strategy [**8.6(d)**]?
6   Assess the possibility that Carranza [**8.7**] belonged to the 'third party' [**3.17**].
7   What impression of 16th-century Spain is given by **8.1–8.7**?

II Competing religions: Counter Reformation in the Empire before 1618

The Peace of Augsburg (1555) was a pragmatic truce which constructed a remarkable peace. Protestantism held the upper hand. Catholicism as it emerged from the Reformation's first 40 years 'seemed like a lost cause' (Po-Chia Hsia, 1989). But Augsburg threw a safety net under the remaining Catholic states and ushered in 30 years of peaceful co-existence. Everything began to change from the 1570s as the Empire 'confessionalised' – split up again into rival religious camps. Among Protestants, the new dynamic was provided by militant Calvinism. Yet it was primarily the Catholics who prospered. All along the front line, which stretched from the Rhineland through Franconia and Swabia into Carinthia, Styria and up into Bohemia, whole states were brought home. Between 1570 and 1618, the proportion of the imperial population which was Catholic doubled to about 60 per cent.

How was this counter-thrust achieved? First, political support provided the environment for recovery and renewal: 'Princes now became not merely arbiters, but the counter-reformers of their countries' (Trevor-Roper, 1985). The confessional state was as much a Catholic as a Protestant phenomenon. Among rulers who resolutely asserted their right under the 1555 Peace to determine the religious allegiance of their subjects, Bavarian dukes and (later) Austrian archdukes usually get the credit. But the reassertion of Catholicism was not dependent on secular rulers alone. Also important were a swathe of prince bishops and abbots like Münster, Constance, Salzburg and Fulda. Nor should we overlook Gregory XIII (1572–85), who set the empire at the top of the papal Counter Reformation agenda, selecting with great care the nuncios sent to princely and episcopal courts to inspire, cajole and direct Catholic renaissance. The alliance of church and state, a relationship of mutual dependence and benefit, was never a partnership of equals. Catholic rulers pursued their own particular interests with skilled tenacity, using religious questions to bolster their own political pre-eminence; contemporary wisdom itself believed that heresy was the prime cause of rebellion: 'pure religion was becoming ever less significant as a factor in determining policy' (Spitz, 1980).

Second, those princes sponsored missions to stabilise the old religion, to convert Protestant subjects and to secure the confused. The single-minded objective was to enforce confessional conformity across a state. Capuchins and Jesuits were almost invariably summoned from outside to settle and proselytise. Both started from the premise that all but the leading Protestants were misguided, and so in need of assistance not punishment. Their weapons were gentle: sermons and books, catechisms and hymns, plays and processions; there was no Inquisition. Mission was targeted very precisely against towns and large villages of mixed or Protestant population and aimed to win confidence and affection. It was a policy of infiltration and the results were spectacular. By the 1590s, Central European Catholicism was assertive and would soon become aggressive. The long truce had been used to real effect. Catholicism held the upper hand.

8.8   Catholic safe-havens

16. Estates espousing the Augsburg Confession shall let all the Estates and Princes who cling to the old religion live in absolute peace and in the enjoyment of all their estates, rights and privileges ...

18. Where an archbishop, bishop or prelate or any other priest of our old religion shall abandon the same, his archbishopric, bishopric, prelacy, and other 5
benefices, together with all their income and revenues which he has so far possessed, shall be abandoned by him without any further objection or delay. The chapters and such as are entitled to it by common law or the custom of the place shall elect a person espousing the old religion, who may enter on the possession and enjoyment of all the rights and incomes of the place without any further 10
hindrance ...

23. No Estate shall try to persuade the subjects of other Estates to abandon their religion nor protect them against their own magistrates ...

The Peace of Augsburg, September 1555, in Kidd, *Documents,* **pp. 363–4**

8.9   To admit the Jesuits? Rival Catholic agendas

8.9(a)

Since we do not have full jurisdiction in the city and already the council and citizens, followers of the Augsburg Confession, have appointed preachers, it might well happen (since not everyone likes to accept everything with tolerance), especially if it were a Jesuit college [established], they will lead each other to

disputation and other troubles, and this might cause all sorts of divisions ... even   5
unneighbourly behaviour by the elector.

The Bishop of Speyer, 1566

8.9(b)

His Lordship does not have an enclosed principality as others do, and is not as
strong and powerful as some other Catholic princes, but instead is surrounded on
all sides by electors and nobles of other religion ... For the time being,
unfortunately, it is necessary to remain good neighbours ... until a general council
can bring both sides to a unified understanding ... We must [therefore] proceed   5
and negotiate with care.

The Bishop of Speyer, 1578

8.9(c)

Because the almighty God has now shown us this way [a Jesuit college], through
which not only the pulpits but also the schools would be served properly, the
Christian religion built up, restored, and spread, services preserved ... My lords
[the canons] do not consider the founding a little thing to be passed over lightly,
but instead they want to put spiritual before temporal ones ... We feel it is a good   5
Christian work, which should contribute to the preservation of religion and
worship.

The cathedral chapter of Speyer, 1565

All extracts from M. Forster, *The Counter-Reformation in the Villages:*
Religion and Reform in the Bishopric of Speyer, 1560–1720, **Cornell**
University Press, Ithaca, 1992, pp. 48, 45, 68–9

8.10   Mission as Counter Reformation

My brothers, a sacred task is laid upon you. Remain steadfast in that calling ...
You are called to do battle with wicked lies that have brought a once mighty state
into the dust and damned countless souls to eternal torment. Search out heresy
and by your skill show its false foundations. Seek out heretics and by your
eloquence soften their hearts to receive the ancient truth of their forefathers.   5
Make them your burden and your joy. Heal them, else they die.

The Capuchin Provincial in Austria, 1593, in J. Lünig, *Continuatio*
Spicilegii Ecclesiastici, **Leipzig, 1720, p. 186†**

Questions

1   Explain the significance of clause 18 ('The Reservation') in **8.8**.
2   (a)   'Until a general council' [**8.9(b) line 4**]. What do you make of such a statement 15 years after Trent?
    (b)   Of what was the bishop afraid in **8.9(a)** and **8.9(b)**?
    (c)   Assess how far **8.9(a)–(c)** show there was no longer agreement about what the Peace of Augsburg stood for.
3   How does the mission in **8.10** differ from those in Chapter 6?
4   How far do **8.9** and **8.10** show:
    (i)   a recovery of Catholic confidence?
    (ii)   that the peaceful co-existence of 1555 was destroyed by the Catholic side?

The Jesuits

Jesuits have always been recognised as central to Counter Reformation. As theologians, their commitment to Thomism helped mould Trent's sharp rejection of Augustinian salvation theology and compromise with Protestantism. Thereafter, they dominated the intellectual battle, producing a torrent of good books which inspired devotion or mercilessly revealed theological inconsistencies and scholarly errors among opponents. As preachers, their pastoral and doctrinal work was of the utmost importance. As teachers, their schools and colleges promoted a positive Catholic image and confessional conflict, both invaluable in Reformation frontier towns like Mainz, Lucerne and Olomouc. Indeed, so good (and so cheap) was Jesuit education that Protestants sent their sons in increasing numbers and classrooms became powerful instruments of Counter Reformation. In consequence, the Catholic elite of the next generation was possessed of a spirit quite different to that of their parents: articulate, confident and ultramontane (looking to Rome for leadership); one-third of 17th-century German bishops were Jesuit-educated. The tolerance of Augsburg was doomed. The divisions were hardening. A new militancy stalked Christendom.

Jesuit mission strategy often targeted the well-to-do and the influential, focusing sharply on all levels of government. As confessors to princes, they became infamous for the political control they were said to wield. This has been much exaggerated. Jesuit 'advisers' at such courts certainly exercised considerable influence in ecclesiastical matters. Sometimes they were drawn into unpopular, questionable, even factional matters. That was inevitable, given the impossibility of defining precisely what distinguished 'the interest of the church' or 'the conscience of the prince' from 'external and political matters' (The Jesuit Father-General, 1602). But Jesuits were criticised whatever they did. Wherever they went among their co-religionists, they aroused deep envy and petty jealousy. Philip II thought them too papal; France and several popes thought them too Spanish. They were accused of preaching absolutist monarchy, tyrannicide and republicanism. Why? They pursued their own agenda. Wherever they settled, they never integrated. They were too independent, too international.

8.11   A strategy for Germany

Our Society should make use of the following means to put a stop and apply a remedy to the evils which have come upon the Church ... exerting itself to the utmost of its powers to preserve what is still sound and to restore what is fallen sick of the plague of heresy ... [Regarding] the sound theology which is taught in the universities ... it would be good to make a summary to deal with topics that   5
are important but not controversial ... It should solidly prove dogmas with good arguments from Scripture, tradition, the councils, and the doctors, and refute the contrary teaching. It would not require much time to teach such a theology, since it would not go very deeply into other matters. In this way, theologians could be produced in a short time ... Another excellent means for helping the Church in   10
this trial would be to multiply the colleges and schools of the Society ... The better among our students could be sent to teach Christian doctrine on Sundays and feast days. Thus by the correct doctrine, they would be giving example of a good life, and by removing every appearance of greed they will be able to refute the strongest argument of the heretics – a bad life, namely, the ignorance of the   15
Catholic clergy. The heretics write a large number of booklets and pamphlets, by means of which they aim at taking away all authority from the Catholics ... It would seem expedient, therefore, that Ours also write answers in pamphlet form, short and well written, so that they can be produced without delay and bought by many ... We should use the same diligence in healing that the heretics are using in infecting the people.

Ignatius Loyola to St Peter Canisius, August 1554, in Young, *Letters of St Ignatius,* **pp. 345–7**

8.12   Tactics

8.12(a)

Teachers will proceed with the greatest moderation against heretics, especially in Germany and France, employing no vituperation against them. Though they most certainly are heretics, they should not be called so, but those of the Augsburg Confession should be called Protestants, the rest, according to their

sects, Anabaptists, Zwinglians ... They ought to use every effort to bring it about   5
that heretics may have no complaint against them save their steadfastness in the
Faith and its defence, and their keen opposition to heresy.

**Order from the Jesuit Father-General, 1580, taken from W. H. McCabe,
An Introduction to the Jesuit Theatre with permission of the Institute of
Jesuit Sources, St Louis, Missouri, 1983, p. 28**

8.12(b)

Try to be on good terms with those in government positions and be kindly
disposed toward them. It will help to achieve this if the duke and the members of
his household who have a wider influence confess to Ours ... Win over the
doctors of the university and other persons of authority by your humility,
modesty, and obliging services. Consequently, if you should learn that you or the   5
Society is in ill esteem, especially with persons in authority, you should prudently
undertake a defense, and try to get them to understand the work of the Society.

**Ignatius Loyola to the Jesuits in Bavaria, September 1549, in Young,
Letters of St Ignatius, p. 213**

8.12(c)

Engage heretics in conversation whenever and wherever the opportunity presents
itself. Remember, Our Lord and his Apostles spoke to the common people in
their houses, in the market place or by the well and told them of the Gospel. If
Our Lord did not confine his preaching and teaching to consecrated places, you
need not worry about it either. In the struggle against heresy, every opportunity   5
is useful and will be consecrated by God ... So prepare yourself with homely
phrases and the daily language of the streets. You go as God's messenger, not as
a schoolroom lecturer.

**Paul Hoffaeus, Jesuit Provincial in South Germany, *Instructiones
Praedicationis Verbi Dei*, Cologne, 1602, p. 21†**

8.13   A new German priesthood

You have heard more than once of the German College which is to be built here
in the city of Rome. It will undertake the education and moral training of
selected young men of good character who give promise of fruits of Christian
piety and virtue ... When they have made creditable progress in learning and
virtue, they will be sent back to Germany and given ecclesiastical benefices.   5
Indeed, those who have been conspicuous for special attainments in virtue will be
promoted to bishoprics and the highest dignities. Those who are intensely
interested in the saving of Germany see in this college the surest and almost only

means to support the tottering and – alas that we should have to say so, of many places at least – the collapsed Church in Germany. It is hoped that very many   10
faithful and energetic young men of that nation and tongue can be sent here, who by the example of a life of study and the influence of their solid learning will preach the word of God, and by their lectures, or at least by their personal influence, will be able to open the eyes of their fellow countrymen.

Ignatius Loyola to the Jesuit Claude Le Jay, in Bavaria, July 1552, in Young, *Letters of St Ignatius*, p. 259

Questions

1 (a) Suggest reasons why **8.11** recommends 'controversial' theology be avoided [**line 6**].
   (b) Explain Ignatius Loyola's call in **8.11** for less theology in clerical training.
2 Detail the ways in which **8.11** and **8.12** reveal how Jesuits:
   (i) reached ordinary people
   (ii) sought the support of the influential.
3 Compare the aims of **8.13** and **8.11**. Had St Ignatius changed his mind on the type of clergy required? Justify your answer.
4 Is the plea for moderation [**8.12(a) lines 1–2**] the same as the call to proceed with care [**8.9(b) lines 5–6**]?
5 From **8.11–8.13**:
   (a) How did St Ignatius explain Protestant success? Was he right?
   (b) How did he aim to combat Protestant heresy?
   (c) Assess how far Jesuit strategy and tactics show that the weaknesses of German anti-reformation (see Chapter 3) had been grasped.
   (d) Consider how faithful these Jesuits were to their *Prima Summa* [**2.11**].
6 Explain why Jesuit colleges could be portrayed 'as the Trojan Horse at Germany's gate' (Cardinal Morone, 1573).

III   Venice and the papacy, 1605–7

Enhanced concepts of the rights of kings and ancient papal claims to universal jurisdiction had embedded friction within the church–state relationship well before the Reformation. Catholic princes were concerned to curb independent ecclesiastical power as much as their Protestant neighbours, and were at least as successful in shifting the balance in their favour. As we here examine the most spectacular of post-medieval confrontations between those competing sovereignties, it is essential not to distinguish in some modern way between religion and politics or think that church and state were then separate. Instead, we must see the question as they did in terms of rival conceptions of order and authority within Christendom. Spiritual and temporal power belonged together, but were they vested in pope or prince? For 600 years and more, both had argued their claim. Princes in the 15th and 16th centuries secured a firm grip upon both spiritual and temporal authority. Within the church, that very same fusion had, as we saw in Chapter 5, produced a newly resurgent papal monarchy, a leadership strengthened by reviving spiritual and intellectual Catholic force. Internal recovery masked for some time, however, the reality of the external position. Late-medieval popes had surrendered considerable ground and their post-Tridentine successors discovered the very processes of Catholic renewal and Counter Reformation only encouraged further secular encroachments. Trent had not, could not have imposed a strait-jacketed, papal-controlled theocracy across Catholic Christendom.

The Venetian Republic was the sole surviving Italian city state and as such was ferociously protective of its ancient liberties. Across the 16th century, there had been periodic disputes with Rome over issues like clerical immunity from taxation or restrictions on the building of monasteries. In 1605, a new row erupted over the arrest of two priests, one for murder and rape, the other for attempted rape. Again, the question was unexceptional: was the Venetian state competent to judge them? Yet this affair was turned into an epic clash between the specific spiritual jurisdictions of the papacy and another Catholic state. Why? The key lies with Paul V (1605–21), a politically inexperienced pope more jealous than most in protecting papal dignity, a lawyer notorious for his inflexibility and a prince concerned to bolster the papacy's political position within Italy. Where his predecessors had known better than to corner a state as prickly as Venice, Paul V decided on a showdown. Venice would be used as a test case, but for what? Clearly the pope thought in terms of the suburban politics of Italy. Certainly he acted in defence of spiritual prerogatives and hoped thereby to caution others. But was Paul also acting on behalf of 'the authoritarian, rigid world of the Counter Reformation to crush its rival: the flexible political, intellectual and cultural values of Renaissance republicanism' (Bouwsma, 1968)? If Bouwsma is correct, the Interdict was another Thomist attack upon the secularised (and therefore amoral) politics Rome associated with Machiavelli – just like the campaign for native rights.

Paul imposed an interdict which excommunicated the entire state, closed its churches and forbade all services. In response, the republic declared the decree invalid. Three religious orders supported Rome and were expelled: the Capuchins, Jesuits and Theatines – was it pure coincidence that all were new Catholic Reformation societies? Their priests were rarely Venetians, unlike the local bishops and parish clergy, but while some of these had to be bullied into compliance, the state's success 'in keeping the mass of the clergy under control was remarkable' (Bouwsma, 1968). At the same time, Venice waged a skilful propaganda war to justify its stance and secure foreign support. Holland and England made noises about a grand coalition against the papacy. The Catholic powers, however, divided by bitter Franco-Spanish rivalry but unwilling and unprepared for European war, were deliberately cautious and limited themselves to jockeying for position in Italy. Spain in particular played a double game of encouraging Rome to stand firm (over papal rights it denied within its own territories) while failing conspicuously to respond to Paul's requests for troops. One year on, the pope was left with no option but to back down. Venice surrendered none of its laws. The Jesuits were not readmitted until 1657. In the full glare of international publicity, the terrible medieval weapon of Interdict had failed. It was a humiliating defeat for the papal prince and for Roman centralisation.

The Venetian case

8.14(a)

We do not understand how it can be possible to suggest that a state like our republic, born in freedom and sustained in its liberty by God for 1200 years, should not be allowed to take those steps which it thinks necessary to preserve itself when those steps in no way prejudice or do harm to the government of other states and princes.

The Venetian Senate to its ambassador in Rome, November 1605

8.14(b)

Princes have authority by divine law to make laws and exercise government in all temporal affairs and concerns within their own sovereign jurisdictions. Since the matters raised by Your Holiness are not spiritual but concern lands and goods within this Republic and belonging to its citizens, there is no occasion for Your Holiness to send here a brief requiring that this state annul decrees duly considered.

The Venetian Senate to Paul V, January 1606

Both extracts from A. Segarizzi, *Relazioni degli Ambasciatori Veneti*, Bari, 1912, pp. 93, 112†

8.14(c)

His Holiness has closed his ears to the most legitimate rights of this Most Serene
Republic and has instead issued a public monitory,[1] contrary to all reason and
against the doctrine of the Holy Scriptures, the Fathers and sacred canon law,
which prejudices the secular authority and sovereign liberty granted to this state
by God, and which threatens the peaceful possession of blessing, and thereby   5
gives scandal to the whole world ...

[1] The Interdict, April 1606.

Edict of the Doge to the Republic's clergy, May 1606, in P. Molmenti,
***Venice, its Growth from the Earliest Beginnings*, London, 1906, IV, p. 121**

The Papal case

8.15   Trent and the duty of princes

The holy council, desirous that ecclesiastical discipline be not only restored
among Christian people, but also forever preserved unimpaired against all
obstacles ... has deemed it proper that secular princes also be admonished of their
duty; being confident that as Catholics whom God has willed to be protectors of
the holy faith and the Church, they will not permit their officials or inferior   5
magistrates through any spirit of covetousness or imprudence to violate the
immunity of the Church and of ecclesiastical persons ... Hence it admonishes the
emperor, kings, states, princes, and each and all, of whatever state or dignity they
may be, that the more bountifully they are adorned with temporal goods and with
power over others, the more religiously should they respect those things that are   10
of ecclesiastical right as ordinances of God and as covered by His protection; and
that they suffer them not to be infringed.

Decree of the Council of Trent, December 1563, in Schroeder, *Canons and
Decrees***, pp. 251–2**

8.16   Church and state: the theory of indirect papal power

The temporal and ecclesiastical are parallel commonwealths, but the temporal is
not autonomous within its own sphere ... The temporal must remain subject to
the spiritual. The pope must be able to do anything necessary for the
preservation and administration of spiritual affairs. He may not have direct power
to control temporal affairs but, to achieve the spiritual goals of Christ's Church,   5
he has indirect powers of jurisdiction over all princes ... He can coerce kings,
especially heretical ones, with the ecclesiastical penalties of excommunication and
even interdict. Should it be necessary, his powers extend to the coercing of kings
with temporal punishments, even with the deprivation of their kingdoms, for by

direct command of Our Lord, it falls to the pope to tend the sheep, to chase   10
away the wolves, to chastise wanderers and bring them back into the fold.

Francisco Suárez, a Jesuit, *A Defence of the Catholic and Apostolic Faith,*
1613, Naples, 1872, I, pp. 281–3, 286–7†

8.17   Indirect power denied

The Fathers are at one with the Scriptures. When Christ lived as man on earth,
he neither accepted nor wanted any temporal dominion, but accepted and
submitted himself to Pilate and to Caesar. As Vicar of Christ, the pope must be
limited in the very same way. He cannot have indirect powers, extensive or
otherwise, to attain the spiritual ends of the church.

Cardinal Bellarmine, a Jesuit, *A Treatise on the Power of the Supreme
Pontiff,* **1610, in** *Opera omnia,* **1870, II, p. 148†**

8.18   Divine right theory

The power of princes may be acquired in any of four ways, by election, heredity,
donation, or conquest in a just war, all of which titles are certainly not divine but
human ... Herein lies the great difference between the ecclesiastical power of the
Pope and the political power of secular princes. The Pope's right to command all
Christians is not based only on the general ordinance of God, in virtue of which   5
obedience is due to every legitimate superior, but also on the fact that God has
given him immediately all Christians as his subjects; for though the Pope is
elected by the cardinals, it is not the cardinals but God who gives him his power
... Kings and secular princes, on the other hand, may lose their subjects entirely
or in part. They can even themselves alienate one of their cities or provinces, and   10
place it under the control of another prince ... But no one can diminish or take
away the power of the Supreme Pontiff.

Cardinal Bellarmine, *Riposta alle oppositioni di Fra Paulo servita,* **Rome,**
1606, in *Opera omnia,* **1870, II, pp. 63–5†**

8.19   A secret agenda?

If you look closely, abuses [referred to by defenders of Venice] are such questions
as clerical celibacy, the sacrifice of the mass and the invocation of saints ... When
they tell you that these abuses directly hinder your salvation, what can those
words mean except that salvation is impossible within the Roman Church? ...
Beware of the real goal of those who guide the Most Serene Republic in these   5
days. Should they succeed in their object, God forbid, they will wreck not just

the faith of that state but, more than likely, its temporal position and the wealth
which depends so closely on that faith ... By the aid of the most Blessed Queen
of Angels and the glorious Evangelist St Mark, I pray that the cunning of the
devil shall not succeed for otherwise heresy shall be admitted, to the ruin first of   10
your ancient Republic, then of Italy.

Cardinal Bellarmine, *Riposta alle oppositioni*, p. 57†

8.20   A papal hidden agenda?

Monarchy offers a government which is more ordered than democracy. Order
consists in one fundamental – that some command and that others obey, the
former being superior, the latter inferior. Monarchy fulfils that requirement to
perfection since all are subject to the one who has responsibility for all. That is
why the church is so ordered: people subject to parish priests, parish priests to   5
bishops, bishops to the pope ... Order is wanting in a democracy for all citizens
share in government. Such a form, depending on no single will, can bring only
confusions, delays, defects.

Cardinal Bellarmine, *De potestate pontificis*, 1607, in *Opera omnia*, 1870, II,
p. 146†

Questions

1   (a)   Explain what Venice thought it was defending [**8.14**].
    (b)   Consider whether she could claim to have been fulfilling Trent
          [**8.15**].
2   (a)   From **8.14–8.16**, explain how papal and Venetian concepts of the
          church–state relationship differed.
    (b)   Were they in any way compatible? Justify your answer.
3   'St Robert was the brightest star of the Jesuit school of theology'
    (Brodrick, *Robert Bellarmine*, 1961)
    (a)   What does **8.17** say about the claims in **8.16**?
    (b)   Does **8.17** invalidate those claims? Explain your answer.
4   (a)   What in **8.14(b)** provoked the writing of **8.18**?
    (b)   To what extent was divine right theory a key issue?
5   (a)   What does **8.19** suggest is the 'real goal' [**line 5**]?
    (b)   Can this be relevant to the dispute?
    (c)   'As Rome realised it was losing, its propaganda became cynical and
          opportunistic' (Bouwsma, *Venice and the Defence of Republican
          Liberty*, 1968). Consider whether **8.19** sustains that claim.

6   'The Tridentine decree on the princes is worded so vaguely that popes
    can use it to justify anything' (Paolo Sarpi, *History of the Council of Trent*,
    1619).
    (a)   What can you find out about Sarpi to explain why he should say
          that?
    (b)   From **8.14–8.19**, consider whether Sarpi was nonetheless correct.
7   Do you think **8.16** and **8.18–8.20** support Bouwsma's thesis that repub-
    licanism was the object of attack? Justify your answer.

IV   Philip II: champion-in-chief of Counter Reformation?

Philip II, his aims and character, remain enigmatic. His motives continue to
perplex scholars as much as they did his contemporaries. Was he prudent or
indecisive? Was his steadfastness of purpose the product of ideological commitment or dim-witted stupidity? Above all, can we take seriously his claim
to have waged a life-long battle with heresy in the service of the faith?
Spaniards of the 16th century presumed they were a people divinely chosen
to save Catholicism. As their king, was Philip the prince among Counter
Reformation warriors? The particular difficulty in judging his motives
derives from one fundamental: 'neither Philip nor his ministers had any
overall political plan' (Koenigsberger, 1971). His conduct of foreign affairs
was not dictated by defined policies and specific aims, but guided by general attitudes and opinions, such as a marked preference for peace, a determined loyalty to the Catholic faith of his ancestors and a reluctance to
become entangled in the affairs of territories and subjects other than his own.
    Every pope during his long reign regarded his talk of 'the preservation of
the Catholic religion' as 'a pretext to safeguard and increase his dominions'
(Sixtus V, 1589). What did Rome have against him? Why could that same
pope regard Spanish victories as a little less disastrous than Spanish defeats?
Popes had nightmares about a Spanish hegemony over the Catholic world
and looked to the revival of France as a counter-balance. Philip's concept of
kingship as a divine commission and his conviction that the interests of
Spain and the Catholic Church were one and the same were both found
intolerable in Rome. He did indeed believe himself to be the force of
heaven's angry flame and thus inevitably characterised his opponents as the
adversaries of God. But then, so too did the papacy. That was why, even
allowing for two virulently anti-Spanish popes, relations between Madrid
and Rome were so consistently appalling that historians have questioned the
possibility of considering 'the forces of the Counter Reformation as though
they were a crusading alliance between Spain and the papacy' (Lynch, 1991).

Not only were they divided over the decidedly subordinate position in which Philip kept the Spanish church and the best tactics for dealing with Ottoman infidels or English heretics. They disagreed fundamentally over the nature of their relationship, neither prepared to play second fiddle.

Strategy in the Netherlands was the only area that never provoked significant disagreement, and so makes for an admirable case study of Philip's motivation. Remember that since for him it was the ends that mattered (not the means), it was aspiration – Philip's vision of those ends – which would determine his behaviour. In a man driven by general maxims rather than formulated policies, that explains much that otherwise seems inconsistent. On the political status of the Low Countries, Philip was extraordinarily flexible, being prepared in 1576 to cede virtually full political control to the States. Religious concessions were, however, a different proposition. He was determined never to accept the principles of the 1555 Peace of Augsburg for to do so would be to admit heretics as subjects, the Netherlands being technically a province of the Empire. Beyond theology and morality, recent experience in France and Scotland showed Philip that Calvinism 'provided the nobility with an instrument ready-made to contest the authority of the state' (Lovett, 1986). Philip's consistent refusal to tolerate Dutch Protestantism served also to defend a political rule of thumb: to preserve intact his patrimony. Even in the Low Countries, religion and politics were thus ultimately entangled within Philip's mind.

Heretics who were not his subjects were approached in quite a different spirit. While he found Protestantism detestable, Philip recognised his limited resources and his primary duty to preserve the health of his own domains. If any act brought them disadvantage, such as papal attempts to depose Elizabeth I in the 1560s, he would have nothing to do with it (and instead used his influence to secure an easier lot for English Catholics). When, however, English meddling in the Netherlands produced a military alliance with the rebels in 1585 and jeopardised the total victory Parma's troops had all but delivered, Philip rushed with 'reckless determination' (Parker, 1977) to launch the Armada.

Protestants talked of a grand coalition of Catholic powers, led by the pope. They misunderstood reality within post-Tridentine Catholicism as much as the popes did. Neither Madrid nor Rome was able to conceive of the possibility that the other could want to do anything but look to it for guidance. Rome deluded itself in thinking that Catholic princes might once again follow a papal monarchy; this battle for command in the field had been lost by the 12th century. Like his fellow princes, Philip would support the church, but he would not serve it.

Philip and the papacy

8.21   King and pope – Philip's view of their relationship

Princes have always held and exercised the right to put their counsels to popes
and to ask what they should do for the benefit and preservation of Christendom.
In their turn, popes have always shown great deference to and respect for those
opinions. In the present state of extreme danger to our holy mother, there are
innumerable reasons why His Holiness should listen to me, listen to my opinions   5
and accept my advice with that same care and respect which his predecessors
showed to me and my illustrious father in similar situations.

**Philip II to Sixtus V, March 1587, in J. de Hübner, *Sixte-Quinte*, Paris,
1882, II, pp. 21–2†**

8.22   Philip upbraids the pope

It is with the greatest surprise that I see Your Holiness, after taking action that
was inspired by God against Henry of Navarre[1] at the beginning of your
pontificate, has allowed heresy to take root in France, without compelling the
Catholic supporters of Navarre to separate from him. The Church is in danger of
losing one of her most prominent members, the whole of Christendom is   5
threatened by the reunited heretics, and Italy is exposed to the gravest dangers.
While the enemies of God are thus advancing you are content to look on and let
things be. I, on the other hand, who look upon all these interests as my own, and
who have recourse to Your Holiness as a beloved and venerated father, and who
as a good son call your attention to the duties of the Holy See, receive in return   10
nothing but insults! Heaven and earth are witnesses of my veneration for the
Holy See. Nothing shall lead me astray on that matter, not even the absurdities
which Your Holiness ascribes to me. But the greater my attachment is, all the
less will I suffer Your Holiness to violate your duties to the Church and to God,
who has given you the means of taking action. At the risk of being importunate   15
and of giving displeasure to Your Holiness, I shall insist upon your setting your
hand to this work. In the event of your not doing so, I shall disclaim all
responsibility for the fatal consequences that will ensue. By this present letter I
wish to defend the Church. I shall believe in the affection which Your Holiness
says that you feel for me, when I see from your actions that Your Holiness is   20
following my advice, paying heed to my prayer, and seriously turning your
attention to remedying the sufferings of France, which so closely affect the whole
of Christendom. If Your Holiness, in correspondence with your duty, and the
assurances which you have so often made, will act in this way, I will lend my aid
as your devoted son.

[1] His excommunication, in September 1585.

Philip to Sixtus, June 1589, in Pastor, *History of the Popes*, XXI, pp. 366–7

8.23   Pope and king – the papal view of their relationship

We are not the slave of your king. We do not owe him obedience, nor are we
accountable to him for our actions. We are his father, and it is not the place of
sons to give him their advice without being asked for it. Do you, who wear a
sword at your side, do you pretend to understand theology better than we do,
who have studied both theology and other sciences? By what right do you come   5
here during the heats of August to molest and threaten us?

Sixtus to Philip's ambassador, August 1590, in Pastor, *History of the*
Popes, **XXI, pp. 369–70**

8.24   The pope upbraids Philip

How can the expedition against England succeed while your Majesty remains in a
state unreconciled with God and his Church? No sin displeases the Almighty
more than the usurpation of ecclesiastical jurisdiction ... Your Majesty has been
advised to include in your recent pragmatica[1] the reservation of all ecclesiastical
titles within your territories, even of bishops, archbishops and cardinals, to the   5
crown. This is a very grave sin. You must remove such clauses from the
pragmatica and do penance forthwith, otherwise some divine punishment will
befall you. Trust no one who advises you in any contrary way, but put your trust
in me, the father given you by God. Believe in this Holy See, your mother, to
which you are bound for your very salvation ... I have shed many tears over this   10
your great sin, praying that you will mend your ways and that God will pardon
you. In matters of salvation, you must obey the Vicar of Christ without reply and
in this hope I pray for every blessing upon your excellent Majesty.

[1]A royal decree. This one dated from October 1586.

Sixtus to Philip, August 1587, in Hübner, *Sixte-Quinte*, **III, pp. 236–7†**

Questions

1   What do you think Philip means by his second sentence in **8.21**?
2   How according to **8.21** and **8.22** would Philip know whether the pope
    violated his 'duties to the Church and to God' [**8.22** line 14]?
3   'God established two governments in the world, one spiritual, one
    temporal. Each is full independent of the other' (Paolo Sarpi, 1616). How
    far does the evidence here suggest Philip would have agreed?
4   Explain and comment on the papal attitude in **8.23**.
5   (a)   Of what is Philip accused in **8.24**?
    (b)   Does **8.24** show signs of having been influenced by the ideas behind
          8.15 and **8.16**? Explain your answer.

6   Can we take seriously Philip's claim to 'veneration for the Holy See' [**8.22 lines 11–12**] after reading **8.23** and **8.24**? Justify your answer.

Philip and the Netherlands

8.25   Philip's strategy

I intend to settle the religious problem in these states without taking up arms, for I know clearly that to do so would result in their complete destruction. But should everything be impossible to settle as I desire without taking up arms, then I am determined to take them up and go there myself to carry it out. Neither personal danger nor the ruin of these my states, nor of all others which have been   5 left to me, will stop me from doing what a Christian prince ought to do in the service of God, the preservation of the Catholic faith and the honour of the apostolic see.

Philip to Pius V, August 1566, in L. Serrano, *Correspondencia diplomática entre España y la Santa sede*, Madrid, 1914, I, pp. 316-17†

8.26   Philip on toleration

In spite of everything I would regret very much to see this toleration conceded without limits. The first step must be to admit and maintain the exercise of the Catholic religion alone, and to subject themselves to the Roman Church, without allowing or permitting in any agreement the exercise of any other faith whatever in any town, farm or special place set aside in the fields or inside a village ... And   5 in this there is to be no exception, no change, no concession by any treaty of freedom of conscience ... They are all to embrace the Roman Catholic faith and the exercise of that alone is to be permitted.

Philip to the Duke of Parma, August 1585, in G. Parker, *The Dutch Revolt*, Penguin Books Ltd, Harmondsworth, 2nd edn, 1985, p. 223

8.27   A strategic U-turn?

8.27(a)

I have been very pleased to hear that you have already begun to apply canonical remedies, such as having good preachers and pastors, founding good schools and reforming the ecclesiastics in accordance with my instruction and, moreover, publishing the decrees of the Tridentine Council ... As to the proceedings of the inquisitors of Louvain, you must endeavour to support them as well as the others   5

in all that concerns the exercise and administration of their charges. For this
makes for the strength and maintenance of religion. You know the importance of
this and I command you urgently to do in this matter all that is so necessary and
not to agree to any different policy. You know how much I have these things at
heart and what pleasure and satisfaction this will give me ... I cannot refrain from   10
telling you that considering the condition of religious affairs in the Netherlands as
I understand it, this is no time to make any alteration ... Since [heretics]
condemned to die advance to execution not in silence, but as martyrs dying for a
cause you should consider whether they ought not to be executed in secret in
some way ... For the rest I can only thank you for all you propose to me, but   15
assure you that my orders are designed for the welfare of religion and of my
provinces and are worth nothing if they are not obeyed. In this way you can keep
my provinces in justice, peace and tranquillity.

Philip to the Governess-General of the Netherlands, October 1565

8.27(b)

Your advisers saw only two possibilities, namely to take up arms (which would be
very difficult) or to give in on some points, to abolish the inquisition and to
moderate the rigour of the edicts little by little ... [and your letter] ended by
insisting on the necessity for me to make a decision immediately (because
otherwise religion and my lands in the Low Countries would both be in   5
immediate danger of being lost) ... I am certain, Madame my dear sister, that you
can easily imagine the great sorrow this very important matter causes me. What is
at stake is on the one hand the respect for our holy Catholic faith which I have
always had at heart and furthered with due zeal and in accordance with the
obligation I have to maintain it; on the other hand I fear that great difficulties   10
and trouble might come to so many of the honest vassals and subjects whom I
have in the Low Countries ...

I should like to tell you that it is not only because of the necessity to act in
this way (although your arguments are fully justified) that I have, without letting
any other consideration influence my decision, complied with all requests so far   15
as my good conscience and the obligation I have to serve God and to conserve
the holy faith and the state allow me, but also because I am naturally inclined to
treat my vassals and subjects rather with love and clemency than with rigour and
severity.

Taking the various points separately and first of all that about the inquisition,   20
I know how important this is. It is the only means the Church has at her disposal
of making every one live and behave according to her commandments ... If the
inquisition were abolished, this would no longer be possible, and it would seem
that then every one would be permitted to live almost as he likes. However, as
the inquisition was originally introduced into my territories in the Law Courts   25
because there were not enough bishops then and because the persons in charge
were negligent, I feel that the situation is now different. The present bishops are

good pastors and can give their flock the care to which they are entitled ... As the
episcopal jurisdiction is now fully and firmly established,[1] I am content for the
inquisition to cease ... I have always been inclined to treat my vassals and subjects   30
with the utmost clemency, abhorring nothing so much as the use of severity
when things may be remedied in another way. If therefore you see that the
difficulties are being overcome by means of the above-mentioned measures and
that a general pardon would be the final measure to pacify the country, I grant
you permission to give it in the form and way you think best ... My condition,   35
however, is that these leagues and confederations will be broken up and that
those who have been guilty of taking part in leagues, confederations, conventicles
and sects or of breaking the edicts in any other way, do not do this any longer
and will behave in future as is becoming to good Catholics, vassals and subjects
of mine.

[1] 'firmly established' = a new network of 18 dioceses was created in 1559.

**Philip to the Governess-General of the Netherlands, July 1566. Both
extracts from** *Texts concerning the Revolt of the Netherlands*, **ed. E.
Kossmann and A. Mellink, Cambridge University Press, 1974, pp. 54–5,
70–3**

Questions

1   Explain from **8.27(a)** and **8.4** how Philip would settle religious problems
    peaceably [**8.25 line 1**].
2   (a)   What do you think Philip means by 'the welfare of religion and of
          my provinces' [**8.27(a) lines 16–17**]?
    (b)   Does the final sentence of **8.27(a)** show that Philip's prime concern
          was political? Explain your answer.
3   (a)   Find out about the situation in the Netherlands in 1565–6. What had
          happened that explains such a reversal of policy?
    (b)   How substantial were Philip's concessions in **8.27(b)**?
    (c)   Did those concessions exceed the limits outlined in **8.26**?
    (d)   Assess the balance between political and religious considerations in
          8.27(b).
4   By comparing **8.25–8.27** with **8.4–8.7**, do we find that Philip treated
    Dutch heretics more leniently than Spanish heretics?
5   Within days of writing **8.27(b)**, Philip declared before a lawyer that it had
    been extracted from him against his will. Does this episode show he was
    a religious hypocrite and an unscrupulous politician? Justify your answer.

8.28 How Philip wanted to be seen

The figure with a spear (left) is Spain. Religion (drooping figure, right) has dropped the cross and chalice (the cup of the mass), the symbols of salvation. The sea monster (background, middle) represents the Turks, the snakes symbolise Protestantism. This picture was commissioned by Philip II.

Titian, *Spain Coming to the Aid of Religion*, Italian, 1575 (Museo del Prado, Madrid)

A wider vision?

8.29   Philip's early attitude to England

8.29(a)

The evil that is taking place in that kingdom has caused me the anger and
confusion I have mentioned ... but we must try to remedy it without involving
me or any of my vassals in a declaration of war until we have enjoyed the
benefits of peace.

Philip to his ambassador in London, 1559, in C. Martin and G. Parker,
***The Spanish Armada*, Hamish Hamilton Ltd, London, 1988, p. 84**

8.29(b)

English affairs depend so entirely on those of Flanders ... His Holiness has taken
this step[1] without consulting me, which certainly has greatly surprised me because
my knowledge of English affairs is such that I believe I could give a better opinion
upon them, and the course that ought to have been adopted, than anyone else ...
This sudden and unexpected step will exacerbate feeling there, and drive the
Queen the more to oppress and persecute the few good Catholics still remaining.

[1] 'this step' = the excommunication of Elizabeth I.

Philip to his ambassador in London, June 1570, in *Calendar of State*
***Papers Spanish, Elizabeth 1568–79*, London, 1894, p. 254**

8.30   The Armada

8.30(a)

His Majesty was least of all influenced by motives of personal interest, his chief
consideration, indeed his special obligation, being to defend God's cause and end
the outrages committed by England against him ... No step must be therefore
taken by us to interrupt the course of the Divine purpose ... [This war] is so just
it is not to be believed that God will withhold His aid, but that He will favour
the cause even to the utmost of our desires.

Philip to the Duke of Medina Sidonia, July 1588, in 'Documents
Illustrating the History of the Spanish Armada', ed. G. Naish, *The Naval*
***Miscellany*, Navy Record Society, IV, 1952, p. 22**

8.30(b)

If (which God forbid) the result be not so prosperous that our arms shall be able to settle matters, nor, on the other hand, so contrary that the enemy be relieved of anxiety on our account (which God, surely, will not permit) ... there are three principal points upon which you must fix ... The first is that in England the free use and exercise of our holy Catholic faith be permitted to all Catholics, native and foreign, and that those who are in exile be permitted to return. The second is that all the places in my Netherlands which the English hold be restored to me; and the third is that they recompense me for the injury they have done to me, my dominions, and my subjects ... You may point out to them that since freedom of worship is allowed to the Huguenots in France, there will be no sacrifice in allowing the same privilege to Catholics in England.

Philip to the Duke of Parma, April 1588, in *The Great Enterprise*, ed. S. Usherwood, Folio Society, London, 1982, p. 70

Questions

1 (a) How far does **8.28** reflect Philip's view of the temporal–ecclesiastical relationship?
   (b) Assess **8.28** as a source on Philip and Counter Reformation.
2   How characteristic of Philip's attitude to the papacy is **8.29(b)**?
3   From your wider reading, explain Philip's early attitude to Protestant England.
4   If 'English affairs depended so entirely on those of Flanders' [**8.29(b)** line 1], do **8.29–8.30** show the Armada was 'least of all influenced by motives of personal interest' [**8.30(a) line 1**]? Explain your answer.
5   Suggest reasons why Philip would tolerate Protestantism in England [**8.30(b)**] but not in Spain.
6   'To view Spain as the champion of the Counter Reformation is to ignore too many facts' (Lynch, *Spain 1516–1598*, 1991). From the evidence in this section, how far do you agree? Explain your answer.

References

J. Brodrick, *Robert Bellarmine, Saint and Scholar*, Burns & Oates, 1961
J. Elliott, *Imperial Spain, 1469–1716*, Penguin, 1963
S. Haliczer, *Inquisition and Society in the Kingdom of Valencia, 1478–1834*, University of California Press, 1990
H. Kamen, *Golden Age Spain*, Macmillan, 1988
A. Lovett, *Early Habsburg Spain, 1517–1598*, Oxford University Press, 1986
J. Lynch, *Spain 1516–1598: From Nation State to World Empire*, Blackwell, 1991

E. Monter, *Frontiers of Heresy: The Spanish Inquisition from the Basque Lands to Sicily*, Cambridge University Press, 1990

G. Parker, *The Dutch Revolt*, Allen Lane, 1977

L. Spitz, *The Renaissance and Reformation Movements*, Rand McNally, Chicago, 1980

H. R. Trevor-Roper, 'The Culture of the Baroque Courts', in his *Renaissance Essays*, Fontana, 1985

For Bouwsma, Cameron, Po-Chia Hsia and Koenigsberger, see *Suggestions for further reading*.

Suggestions for further reading

The listing here in no way pretends to be comprehensive. My choice has been determined by recent works whose sheer importance or usefulness guarantees them a place, and is influenced by items I have especially enjoyed while researching for this book.

Items marked * are paperbacks.

General surveys

*J. Bossy, *Christianity in the West, 1400–1700*, Oxford University Press, 1985: intriguing overview of beliefs and their impact

*E. Cameron, *The European Reformation*, Clarendon Press, 1991: the most recent grand survey – splendid

J. Delumeau, *Catholicism between Luther and Voltaire: A New View of the Counter-Reformation*, Burns and Oates, 1977: challenged all thinking on this subject

H. O. Evennett, *The Spirit of the Counter-Reformation*, Cambridge University Press, 1968: delightful to read, full of judicious insights

K. von Greyerz (ed.), *Religion and Society in Early Modern Europe, 1500–1800*, George Allen & Unwin, 1984: wide-ranging collection of stimulating essays

A. D. Wright, *The Counter-Reformation: Catholic Europe and the Non-Christian World*, Weidenfeld & Nicolson, 1982: hard-going and by assuming the pattern of Milan was typical of all Catholic Christendom his generalisations are dangerously misleading – read this book *after* you have mastered the subject

Specific works

D. V. N. Bagchi, *Luther's Earliest Opponents: Catholic Controversialists 1518–1525*, Augsburg Fortress Press, 1991: the first major analysis in English of anti-Reformation literature

*J. Bilinkoff, *The Avila of St Teresa: Religious Reform in a Sixteenth Century City*, Cornell University Press, 1989: vivid images of the atmosphere within which reform struggled

R. Bireley, *Religion and Politics in the Age of the Counterreformation*, University of North Carolina Press, 1981: takes Chapter 8, section II onwards into the Thirty Years War – almost a 'whodunnit'

J. Bossy, 'The Counter-Reformation and the Peoples of Catholic Europe', *Past and Present*, XLVII, 1970:   extremely influential

W. J. Bouwsma, *Venice and the Defence of Republican Liberty: Renaissance Values in the Age of the Counter Reformation*, University of California Press, 1968: contentious and difficult in parts, but an exciting story well told

J. Brodrick, *The Origin of the Jesuits* (1940), reissued Loyola University Press, 1986: a classic – the best of curtain-raisers to Ignatius and his Order

W. A. Christian, *Local Religion in Sixteenth Century Spain*, Princeton University Press, 1981:   explains 'popular religion' effortlessly

D. Fenlon, *Heresy and Obedience in Tridentine Italy: Cardinal Pole and the Counter-Reformation*, Cambridge University Press, 1972:   delicate study of the *spirituali*

M. Forster, *The Counter-Reformation in the Villages: Religion and Reform in the Bishopric of Speyer, 1560–1720*, Cornell University Press, 1992:   typifies the local studies now adding so much to our understanding of what actually happened. Use it in conjunction with Po-Chia Hsia (see below)

˙S. Greenblatt, *Marvellous Possessions: The Wonder of the New World*, Clarendon Press, 1991:   exciting examination of European responses to America

B. Hall, 'The Colloquies between Catholics and Protestants, 1539–41', *Studies in Church History*, VII, 1971:   very readable account of reunion schemes, wistfully told

˙R. Po-Chia Hsia, *Social Discipline and the Reformation: Central Europe, 1550– 1750*, Routledge, 1989:   summary of research on the effects of reform – Catholic and Protestant

H. Jedin, *A History of the Council of Trent*, Thomas Nelson, 2 vols., 1957:   the standard work – heavy but highly informative

˙H. Kamen, *Inquisition and Society in Spain in the Sixteenth and Seventeenth Centuries*, Weidenfeld & Nicolson, 1985:   broad evaluation – a corrective to the 'black legend'

H. G. Koenigsberger, 'The Statecraft of Philip II', *European Studies Review*, I, 1971:   investigates Philip's motives – salutary

˙Bartolomé de Las Casas, *A Short Account of the Destruction of the Indies* (1542), Penguin Classics, 1992:   a must – it will make your flesh creep

˙J. McConica, *Erasmus*, Past Masters, Oxford University Press, 1991:   concise yet sensitive introduction to this crucial figure

B. Moeller, 'Piety in Germany around 1500', in *The Reformation in Medieval Perspective*, ed. S. Ozment, University of Chicago Press, 1971:   seminal thesis, stimulating new lines of research

J. W. O'Malley, *The First Jesuits*, Harvard University Press, 1993: comprehensive reassessment of their aims – not a stormtrooper in sight

F. Oakley, *The Western Church in the Later Middle Ages*, Cornell University Press, 1979:   first-rate – rich in suggestions

˙J. C. Olin, *Catholic Reform from Cardinal Ximenes to the Council of Trent, 1495– 1563*, Fordham University Press, 1990:   valuable introduction, followed by excellent documents

*J. Pelikan, *The Christian Tradition: Reformation of Church and Dogma, 1300–1700*, University of Chicago Press, 1984: complex, but invaluable for the theology

P. Prodi, *The Papal Prince, One Body and Two Souls: The Papal Monarchy in Early Modern Europe*, Cambridge University Press, 1987: ground-breaking work on papal government

B. Pullan, *Rich and Poor in Renaissance Venice: The Social Institutions of a Catholic State, to 1620*, Basil Blackwell Publishers, 1971: religious or social history? – you can't always tell the difference now

*J. J. Scarisbrick, *The Jesuits and the Catholic Reformation*, Historical Association, 1988: very brief – exceedingly useful

*H. J. Schroeder, *The Canons and Decrees of the Council of Trent*, TAN Books, Illinois, 1978: the full text of all the legislation

R. W. Scribner, 'Ritual and Popular Religion in Catholic Germany at the Time of the Reformation', *Journal of Ecclesiastical History*, XXXV, 1984: fine article illustrating contemporary approaches

R. W. Scribner, 'Why there was no Reformation in Cologne', in his *Popular Culture and Popular Movements in Reformation Germany*, Hambledon Press, 1987: we need many more studies like this

H. R. Trevor-Roper, *Princes and Artists: Patronage and Ideology at Four Habsburg Courts, 1517–1633*, Thames & Hudson, 1976: art as propaganda – thought-provoking text, superb pictures

H. Tüchle, 'The Peace of Augsburg: New Order or Lull in the Fighting', in *Government in Reformation Europe, 1520–1560*, ed. H. J. Cohn, Macmillan, 1971: clarifies exactly what the famed agreement meant in practice

Index